"This book will help you appreciate the value of your own truth-telling and share it with others. I urge you to read it and live by it."
—**Ken Blanchard**, coauthor, *The One Minute Manager*

"Full of rich experience and wisdom. I heartily recommend it."
—**Freeman Dhority, Ph.D.**, senior partner,
Leading Learning Communities

"Laurie Weiss helps you break the taboo of not admitting the truth on the job by giving you the skills and strategies of truth-telling without damaging yourself or others. She offers important steps to create a supportive organizational culture and helps you experience both the relief and rewards that come with telling the truth."
—**Dorothy Jongeward**, coauthor, *Born to Win*

"Non-threatening, personal, and accessible. Laurie Weiss gives readers the opportunity to draw themselves out without feeling badly. The non-confrontational language makes it work."
—**Lora Vahue**, coach/consultant/writer

"Laurie Weiss gives us a refreshing and realistic statement of the power of truth-telling in business organizations. She makes a compelling case that is tempered by appropriate caution and sophistication—and she maintains a sense of humor and wit that is captivating. This book sets a standard for relationships in modern organizations, whether they be small business concerns, large corporations, or public sector bureaucracies."
—**Robert W. Gage, Ph.D.**, professor of public affairs,
University of Colorado

"Business is an institution that holds truth to be rather low on the totem pole of values. Yet virtually all other institutions—religion, law, philosophy, science, art, psychology—encourage people to speak the truth without prejudice. This book tackles truth-telling in business with great insight and gusto and with marvelous examples. It is high time we took seriously the value of truth and how it applies practically to what after all affects us all—business."

—**Alec Tsoucatos, Ph.D.**, adjunct professor, economics and business, Regis University

"I've been looking for a book like this, a book I can share with my colleagues. The scenarios in each chapter are about real people in real situations described in plain language. Laurie Weiss uses them effectively."

—**Ravi Sethi**, Research Vice President, Computing and Mathematical Sciences, Bell Labs, Lucent Technologies

What Is the Emperor Wearing?

What Is the Emperor Wearing?

TRUTH-TELLING IN
BUSINESS RELATIONSHIPS

Laurie Weiss, Ph.D.

Butterworth–Heinemann
Boston   Oxford   Johannesburg   Melbourne   New Delhi   Singapore

Butterworth–Heinemann supports the efforts of American Forests and the Global ReLeaf program in its campaign for the betterment of trees, forests, and our environment.

Library of Congress Cataloging-in-Publication Data
Weiss, Laurie, 1939–
    What is the emperor wearing? : truth-telling in business relationships / Laurie Weiss.
        p.   cm.
    Includes bibliographical references and index.
    ISBN 0-7506-9872-1 (alk. paper)
    1. Business communication.   2. Interpersonal communication.
    3. Interpersonal relations.   4. Truthfulness and falsehood.
    I. Title.
    HF5718.W443   1998
    650.1'3—dc21   97-17512
                                                                              CIP

British Library Cataloguing-in-Publication Data
A catalogue record for this book is available from the British Library.

The publisher offers special discounts on bulk orders of this book.
For information, please contact:

Manager of Special Sales
Butterworth–Heinemann
225 Wildwood Avenue
Woburn, MA 01801-2041
Tel: 617-928-2500
Fax: 617-928-2620

For information on all Butterworth–Heinemann business books available, contact our World Wide Web home page at: http://www.bh.com

10 9 8 7 6 5 4 3 2 1

Printed in the United States of America

This book is dedicated to the memory of my passionate and generous friend Barbara Bowers

CONTENTS

PREFACE

Almost two decades ago, I served on the board of trustees of an international professional organization that was called upon to review an ethics decision. The issue was tearing the organization apart. The review was made immensely more difficult because many of the trustees, including myself, had been students of the respected senior organization member who had been found guilty of ethical violations.

For months we struggled painfully to understand different interpretations of events that many of us had witnessed directly or been informed about when they occurred. I gradually became aware of how easily I had accepted others' explanations of events instead of evaluating them for myself. I also became convinced that everyone involved believed that they were telling the truth about the events in which they participated. From my perspective, I could understand why each of them could be interpreting the situation as they did.

My fascination with the difficulty of people truly communicating their perceptions to others began when I was only fifteen and an avid science-fiction reader. After reading about General Semantics in A. E. VanVogt's *The World of A* (1948), a friend suggested that I read S. I. Hayakawa's *Language in Thought and Action* (1949). It took all summer, but I finally understood the concept that we can each only perceive a portion of what goes on around us, and that the words we use to communicate about what we perceive describe only a small part of what we have observed. This understanding changed my life.

I was no longer convinced that any description of anything was actually true, because I knew that all abstract words used to describe an event leave out far more information than they include. I understood that, in a sense, we all create our own reality by the choices we make about which bits of information to attend to and which to ignore. Later, as a psychotherapist, I learned how our earliest experiences create the filters through which we view the world, and that they also influence our propensity to select the information that is congruent with our existing belief systems.

My training in Transactional Analysis included exposure to the powerful "passivity material" (Schiff and Schiff 1971), which allows the practitioner to help the client discern the motivation for systematically ignoring important information (denial). It also allows the client to perceive hidden information—the "truth." In order to become proficient in using this material, my husband and I, along with our professional colleagues, made agreements to confront each other when we observed evidence of passive behavior and thinking. We all spent a great deal of time learning hidden truths about ourselves and each other, while increasing our effectiveness as therapists and consultants.

When I taught my organization and business clients this material, they were thrilled with how quickly and easily it allowed them to understand important but confusing situations. Later I discovered that a series of agreements, implemented by some businesses, had a similar effect. Using them kept communication in an organization open, candid, and straightforward, so that everyone's personal perceptions (truths) could be readily shared.

When a group of friends adapted these agreements to create a support group (The Geneva Group) and invited us to participate, we learned even more about how close and respectful relationships are enhanced by sharing our personal truths. My Geneva Group family has been a consistent source of love and support for many years. The agreements we live by with each other, as well as the other tools I have learned that help individuals to know and share the truth, are all included in this book.

For the past quarter century, I have been privileged to assist my clients as they have shared their struggles to learn their own truth and communicate it to others. Some of their stories are included here. Other stories were shared by my friends and colleagues as they learned of this project.

Ten years of service on the ethics committee of the International Transactional Analysis Association have brought me an even deeper perspective on how the inadvertent selection of information to support a favored position can lead to damaged lives and relationships. I have learned how important it is to be able to examine and discuss the assumptions we make, instead of insisting that they are *the truth*.

Truth-telling is a challenge. It is time to start a conversation about the subject. I hope you will use this book to begin to appreciate the value of learning your own truth and sharing it with others—and to engage in the conversation.

Laurie Weiss
Littleton, Colorado
July 1997

References

Hayakawa, S. I. *Language in Thought and Action*. San Diego: Harcourt Brace, 1949.

Schiff, J., and A. Schiff. "Passivity." *Transactional Analysis Journal* 1, no. 1 (1971): 71–78.

VanVogt, A. E. *The World of A*. New York: Simon & Schuster, 1948.

ACKNOWLEDGMENTS

Creating this book has been a joyful and fulfilling experience thanks to the help and support of many people. This book could never have been written without the cooperation of the people whose stories it contains; those who were willing to be known are identified in the text. I cannot thank the others by name, because they have been promised anonymity. You know who you are, and I thank you for your candor, for the long conversations, and for your feedback after the stories were written.

I could not have completed this work without the unwavering support of my business partner, professional colleague, editor, computer expert, travel planner, and caretaker for our geriatric cat. All of these roles are embodied by my husband, Jon Weiss. He encouraged me to take whatever time I needed from our other enterprises while he attended to the many details that keep our lives flowing, despite my inattention.

My daughter, Rachel Weiss Claret, read every word through the critical eyes of an editor, graduate student of management, and small-business owner. She provided many valuable suggestions for improving the clarity of this work, as well as hugs and encouragement whenever I needed them, despite her own busy schedule.

Liz Gardener, ever-faithful manuscript reader and supplier of thoughtful comments and encouragement, always returned my chapters in a timely way and kept my e-mail box full of good jokes. Alec Tsoucatos reviewed the manuscript and challenged my thinking on many critical points. Lora Vahue encouraged me and helped me appreciate myself and the value of my work. Lize Csrnko provided a rapid and thoughtful review of the final manuscript. Manuscript readers Ed Hessek, Roger Frenette, and Fred Rainguet contributed many helpful comments. Members of my Geneva group family offered their unconditional love and support. Special thanks go to Glenn and Marian Head, Gail Hoag, and Joanne Cohen, all of whom contributed information and important insights to this project.

Members of my National Association of Women Business Owners roundtable group and my mastermind group have all offered ongoing encouragement, as well as their own stories.

Others who were not directly involved in the preparation of this work but were nonetheless critical to its development are my teachers Jean Houston, Lawrence (Larry) LeShan, and Howard Bad Hand; they challenged me to be unremittingly honest with myself.

My colleagues who served with me on the Board of Trustees of the International Transactional Analysis Association, in 1978 and 1979, had a major impact on my professional development. They had the courage to examine their own beliefs and prejudices; by doing so they helped to create an environment where all of us, working together, respectfully resolved a very difficult situation.

I also salute my colleagues on the Ethics Committee of the International Transactional Analysis Association with whom I worked for ten years. We learned many lessons together. Without your commitment to compassionate truth-telling, this book would never have been written.

Dena Zocher created order in our office and allowed me to focus my attention on writing.

Stephanie Gelman Aronson of Butterworth–Heinemann provided whatever information, encouragement, and support I needed, just an e-mail away. Karen Speerstra of Butterworth–Heinemann encouraged me to create this book in this form and has offered support and friendship throughout the entire process.

These few words can only begin to express how much I appreciate all of you. Thank you!

Laurie Weiss
Littleton, Colorado
July 1997

INTRODUCTION

Once upon a time, a long time ago, an emperor who loved clothes was approached by two con men who made him an offer he could not refuse. They promised to weave him a special cloth that would be invisible to any people who were stupid or unworthy of their positions. The emperor contracted to have the cloth woven, paying in advance for the special supplies needed. Word rapidly spread about the magical nature of the cloth.

As the work proceeded, the emperor sent high-ranking officials to inspect the looms. Each official in turn observed only empty air where the "weavers" pointed to the rare and beautiful "cloth," and each official grew frightened that only he could not see what others were pointing to. Each reported to the emperor that the work was proceeding well, that the nonexistent cloth

*was magnificent, and that it was appropriate to make addi-
tional payments on the contract.*

*Finally the emperor himself and his entourage came to inspect
the cloth. None could see it, but all (including the emperor),
fearing to be known as stupid or unworthy, proclaimed its
magnificence. The con men pretended to cut and sew the invisible cloth into garments for the emperor to wear in a public
procession. Everyone supported the deception, each fearing that
he or she was the only one who could not see the emperor's
new clothes.*

*A small child, viewing the naked emperor, and perhaps un-
aware of good manners or magical cloth, announced to all who
could hear, "The emperor has no clothes." The chroniclers state
that some of the people echoed the cry of the child, but the
emperor's entourage continued to act as if the emperor was
magnificently dressed.*

The story of the emperor's new clothes is eternal because the
problem is eternal. The benefits of deception are obvious. You can
appear knowledgeable and keep your job. If you trust your own
perceptions enough to share them with others, the risks are considerable. Suppose there really is cloth there and only *you* cannot
see it. Suppose your truth is not the truth. Are there really any
benefits to revealing your truth to others? Are the benefits worth
the accompanying risks?

"I have to live with myself, and so, I want to be fit for myself to
know!" stated a poet who lived in a simpler time. Is it possible to
measure the benefits of knowing that you are maintaining your
own integrity? If the answer to this question were simple and
straightforward, we would not need to wrestle with it. Sometimes
telling the truth as you see it leads to great benefit for everyone
concerned. At other times it leads to disaster. Perhaps the best
answer to this questions is an unqualified "It depends: it depends
on many things."

Most business and professional people agree that telling the
truth is a good idea, yet they routinely practice deception with
each other. Sometimes these deceptive practices are deliberate.
More often they result from self-deception caused by living in a

culture where saving face and looking good are highly valued, and where causing another embarrassment is a painful experience for everyone concerned. Avoiding potential conflict and wanting the rewards of being a team player often cause a retreat from telling "the truth, the whole truth, and nothing but the truth." The process gets even more complicated when you are uncertain about what the truth really is. Unless you discuss it with others, you can only understand it from your own point of view.

Truth-telling is justifiably perceived to be difficult, risky, and unrewarding. Who has not had his or her view of a situation invalidated by someone in authority? Who has not felt ashamed of causing another embarrassment by calling attention to a truth that was supposed to remain a secret? Even as we are fascinated with courtroom drama, hoping to learn the real truth, it becomes apparent that even in court what is true depends on your point of view. When individuals perceive different truths it is far more common to try to invalidate each other's truth than to explore further to discover the true nature of a problem.

Even those who are committed to telling the truth in theory often have difficulty putting the theory into practice. Training in deception abounds. Every child eventually discovers that the toys advertised on television are not magical at home. We are all carefully taught to pretend not to notice certain things. Eventually we no longer need to pretend; we are effectively brainwashed into a cultural trance. We see what we expect to see instead of what is really there. Thus we are protected from accidentally stumbling upon or revealing potentially dangerous secrets.

The first casualty of deception is trust. Lack of trust quickly leads to dysfunctional organizations and relationships. Common symptoms of this problem include miscommunication, frustration, misunderstanding, anger, depression, guilt, distrust, cynicism, hopelessness, mistakes, employee turnover, environmental damage, and a focus on survival instead of learning, growth, and creativity.

Despite the perceived and real risks of truth-telling, in most situations the results are more than worth the risks. Trust develops only where truth-telling is *cherished and nurtured*. When trust exists, synergistic relationships can flourish: businesses report increases in sales, in customer satisfaction, and in innovative ideas

that have lowered costs; work becomes more enjoyable and exciting for everyone, and employee turnover is reduced.

Individuals, relationships, and organizations must all learn and
grow to be successful. As an individual, you need to learn how to
break out of the cultural trance and recognize your own perceptions of the truth before you can become a truth teller. It helps
when you recognize that your truth is not *the truth*, and neither is
anyone else's.

Truth-telling without skillful communication puts the individual at risk of reprisal and worse at the hands of the majority,
who fear new perspectives and change. Training in telling the
truth so another can hear it, and so that the truth teller is not
harmed in the process, is rare. We need to develop skills in both
recognizing truth and communicating it.

If you are trying to decide whether to tell the truth in a business
or professional environment, or if you want to communicate truthfully and do not know how, the stories presented here should
provide food for thought. These are stories of ordinary individuals
in the workplace who are striving to steer a course between deception and damaging confrontation by developing truth-telling
skills. The stories are based on actual events, but in most cases
details have been altered to protect the identity of the individuals
involved.

The first part of this book examines how different individuals
resolved dilemmas when telling the truth seemed difficult or impossible. The second part focuses on stories of individuals who
know how to use tools to help themselves and others tell the truth
with awareness and compassion. As you relate to their struggles
and successes, you will learn the techniques and strategies that
will help you to steer your own course through the treacherous
business environment of the approaching millennium.

THE EMPEROR'S WARDROBE: TALES OF THE TRIALS OF TRUTH-TELLING

Chapter 1: It's Hard to Tell the Truth to Someone Who Won't Listen

Rita was quite certain that Kerwin, her manager, was making a disastrous decision. He refused to listen to her. She tried politely repeating her message several times and finally gave up. Her predictions were correct. Public funds were wasted, and the newspapers uncovered the scandal. Did she have other options?

Chapter 2: It's Hard to Tell the Truth When You Would Rather Not Know What It Is

Robert, the owner of a dry cleaning establishment, could not understand why he was losing money in a store that seemed to be doing lots of business. He was reluctant to accept evidence that his store manager was stealing his supplies.

Chapter 3: It's Hard to Tell the Truth When the Truth Is Bad News

Jennifer is still furious about being squeezed out of her company by being demoted three times. She felt humiliated until she recognized that the same steps had been used to cause others to resign as the company downsized. The people who resigned lost their chance to collect severance pay and other benefits. She refused to be intimidated and left with her dignity and her benefits intact.

Chapter 4: When Truths Collide

Carol believed her secretary's work should meet certain standards and told her so. Her secretary, a member of a minority group, told others that Carol was a "bitch" and threatened to file a discrimination suit. The harder Carol tried to be nice, the worse the situation became.

Chapter 5: I Want to Be a Team Player, so I Won't Make Waves

Fred did not want to think about the financial status of his company. His management team obliged him by not troubling him with the negative information they had accumulated. His belief in his own invulnerability almost cost him his company.

Chapter 6: I Would Be Glad to Tell the Truth If Only I Knew What It Was

Ron was not really aware of the resentment he felt toward his wife, who was also his business partner. He could not tell her the truth, because he had never noticed his own feelings. Instead, he acted out his anger by not keeping agreements he made with her.

Chapter 7: Maybe the Emperor Really Is Wearing Clothes, and I Can't See Them

Marilyn, a new technician, thought she saw the doctor spill a drop of radioactive material on the floor, but she was not quite sure, so she did not speak about it. The radioactive material had indeed spilled, and it took two working days to clean up the contamination in the laboratory. Marilyn did not even share the story until years later.

Chapter 8: Facing Ethical Dilemmas

When Allen was given advance notice that the profitable store he managed was going to close, he was ordered to keep it a secret from his loyal customers and his suppliers. He felt trapped between his responsibility to carry out the wishes of his employer and his personal commitment to integrity.

Chapter 9: Sometimes It Makes Sense Not to Tell the Truth
Marjorie, age forty-eight, probably would have lost her job if anyone learned that she had not actually graduated from high school. Since she was getting outstanding reviews for her work, she decided to keep her secret to herself and continue to work with the difficult clients at a group home for people with special needs.

Chapter 10: Examining Assumptions
Kathleen believed her boss was behaving inappropriately at meetings they attended together. She felt that she could not confront him without jeopardizing her position. When she carefully examined her own discomfort, it dawned on her that her assumptions and objectives might be very different from his.

Chapter 11: Know Yourself First
Irwin, a telecommunications executive, believed that he just could not find good help. One administrative assistant after another resigned after a few days on the job. It never occurred to him that his demanding behavior was contributing to the problem. He was not aware of how radically his behavior changed after he'd had a few drinks with his lunch. The first time a business associate suggested that he might have a problem with alcohol, he did not listen. It took a near disaster to get his attention. Recalling the situation several years later, Irwin identified it as a major turning point in his life and his career.

Chapter 12: Do You Recognize the Signals You Send Yourself?
After five years of helping my business partner/husband produce and market an intensive four-day workshop retreat while maintaining a professional practice and managing our company, I burned out. I felt so depressed that one morning I did not want to get out of bed. That symptom finally got my attention, and I realized that I hated parts of what I was doing. Telling the truth meant risking the destruction of our thirteen-year-old business.

Chapter 13: Use Your Intuition to Guide You

Elizabeth embarrassed herself by occasionally crying at faculty committee meetings. She rarely understood the reason for her tears. Usually she would cry when she was asked to comment on something on which everyone else seemed to agree. When the team hired a consultant, he suggested that the entire group examine the situation more carefully. They discovered that Elizabeth's intuition was warning her when something subtle was wrong with some proposed action.

Chapter 14: The Truth Will Set You Free, but First It May Make You Mad!

Pete reluctantly agreed to hire another consultant to help his executive team clarify what was causing several key professionals to consider resigning from his agency. When several problems were identified, including Pete's inconsistent leadership style, he courageously suggested that the group first focus on his leadership. It was difficult for him to hear the negative feedback, but as he listened and responded, the team members' animosity changed to offers of help and support.

Chapter 15: Get the Information You Need Without Being Gullible or Paranoid

A group of frustrated business owners concluded that "candidates for jobs lie up a storm." Elaine, the president of a temporary staffing agency, agreed, adding that it is hard for people who are "scrambling to try to get decent positions" to be completely truthful about their qualifications. Yet the reputation of her company depends upon creating a good match between the candidate and the prospective employer. She believes it is the job of the interviewer to help candidates tell the truth about themselves so they can be placed where they are most likely to be successful.

Chapter 16: Ask Questions with Grace and Skill

David, a young engineer and team leader at a major electronics firm, used the information he learned at a team development workshop to help his team produce spectacular results. When he was asked to describe his methods at a briefing session for senior management, David first asked questions to get a sense of what he could contribute to their discussion. They were surprised to discover that he was asking about important issues they had not really addressed. Within a year, David became a valued in-house consultant for his company.

Chapter 17: Tell Your Truth with Compassion for Yourself and Others
Valerie struggled with herself about how to inform her client that she suspected he was using drugs. As she prepared him for job interviews, she started to think that other interviewers might notice the subtle symptoms and mannerisms she had observed in him. She carefully examined her own internal conversation and her fear of alienating her client. Her commitment to her own integrity helped her find an appropriate way to take the necessary risk while continuing to support her client.

Chapter 18: All I Did Was . . . Why Did She React That Way?
Judith did not suspect that Marian, her new assistant administrator, was living in the past. Judith knew that Marian responded very poorly to suggestions. Marian was sure that Judith did not like her, and she was ready to resign. Only some careful consultation helped them uncover Marian's truth—that she had Judith confused with her own grandmother.

Chapter 19: Reality Isn't What It Used To Be, and Perhaps It Never Was
Frank, a key employee of a growing electrical contracting company, did not want to believe that times had changed. Although the owner's son, Sam, was getting ready to assume the company presidency, Frank insisted on treating him as if he were still a teenager just learning the business. Sam valued Frank's skill and experience, but he also needed Frank to accept his authority.

Chapter 20: The "What I Feel Like Saying" Process
Staff meetings were becoming a waste of time in Monica's mortgage banking office. Staff members would come late, leave early, and barely pretend to participate. Introducing a simple exercise at the start of each weekly meeting allowed everyone to gradually learn to work together more effectively.

Chapter 21: Is Something Sinister Going On?
Everyone at the meeting was frustrated. People were repeating their points several times, but they were not reaching any resolution. A simple matter that should have taken five minutes had been debated for an hour. After a brief recess, Barry raised a new issue that concerned everyone. When the discussion of the new topic was completed, they went back to considering the original issue, and they reached agreement on a solution almost immediately.

Chapter 22: Using Agreements to Create Dialogue Instead of Conflict
It is important for any truth teller to realize that your truth is not THE TRUTH, and neither is anyone else's. Exploring different perspectives on the truth instead of arguing about which is correct can best be accomplished in a safe environment. A variety of organizations use an ever-evolving set of agreements to create and maintain a context in which truth-telling can occur.

Chapter 23: A Success Story
When Sue found herself in the role of president of the company she and her late husband had started five years earlier, she was overwhelmed. She felt at odds with the whirlwind-paced, crisis-oriented management style her husband had believed was necessary to keep the chaotic business expanding and profitable, but she did not know what else to do. Creating harmony seemed like an impossible dream.

I

PART ONE

Why Not Just Tell the Truth?

"Tell the truth, it's a great shortcut!" proclaims the business card of a counselor. The same idea horrified a group of executives from various companies studying the humanities in a weeklong training program at a prestigious institution. When invited to experiment with being truthful in all their communications for the duration of the program, the executives gave responses that were relatively polite variations of an emphatic NO! Giving up the right to be deceptive was much too threatening. They feared that if they were to do so, they might become vulnerable or somehow compromise business secrets.

Most business and professional people profess to believe in truth-telling and are angry about deceptive practices. Nevertheless, almost everyone will refrain from sharing thoughts and opinions that they believe might embarrass themselves or others. This process, well documented by Chris Argyris of Harvard University (1985), leads to miscommunication, mistrust, and flawed decision making.

Truth-telling certainly can be an invitation to disaster. People agonize about how to share their observations and beliefs, particularly when career advancement, or, indeed, having the opportunity to earn a living at all are at stake. Often it is far easier to live with the status quo rather than risk antagonizing a supervisor or even losing a job by sharing your own beliefs about what is true. Although your unshared truth might contain useful and important information, you keep it hidden to protect yourself.

Even among equals there is always a risk that sharing a view that is different from someone else's will lead to conflict. It is hard to share your own personal experience of what is true when what you say might lead to an unresolvable situation that disrupts a pleasant and rewarding relationship. Few of us are comfortable or skillful in negotiating to resolve the problems that arise when other people express views that differ from our own. Most people do not even realize that there can be many different perspectives on the truth. If someone believes that he or she knows the REAL TRUTH, especially if the person is eloquent about expressing him- or herself, others are often reluctant to engage the person in argument.

Worse still is the possibility of inviting ridicule by expressing your own truth when it's an unpopular point of view. Most people are unwilling to risk telling the truth when being laughed at is a possibility. Childhood experiences of humiliation and embarrassment teach us all to be cautious and protect ourselves. Deciding to speak up for a different position must be weighed against the very real risk of a hurtful response. Many people have great difficulty even believing their own perceptions. Children who are repeatedly invalidated by being told that their observations are incorrect grow into adults who do not trust their own points of view. This is particularly true when alcoholism or violence is present in the home. It is almost impossible to tell your own truth when you are not sure what it is.

Occasionally ethical dilemmas arise wherein telling the truth would cause harm in one area and not telling the same truth might cause harm in another area. Some truths (or secrets) should only be shared when the purpose of sharing them is weighed against the risks of sharing them, and both positive and negative possibilities are clearly understood. Yet most of the deception that causes problems in business and professional relationships results from automatic response patterns we use to protect ourselves without even considering the risks and rewards of telling the truth.

In the chapters that follow we look at the stories of people who have run into problems with telling the truth so that you can begin to understand in a personal way why truth-telling is such a challenge.

Reference

Argyris, C. *Strategy, Change, and Defensive Routines.* Boston: Pitman, 1985.

CHAPTER

1

It's Hard to Tell the Truth to Someone Who Won't Listen

Rita was quite certain that Kerwin, her manager, was making a disastrous decision. He refused to listen to her. She tried politely repeating her message several times and finally gave up. Her predictions were correct. Public funds were wasted, and the newspapers uncovered the scandal. Did she have other options?

As director of community relations of a medium-sized city, Rita had developed a community calendar to educate the public about opportunities to participate in civic affairs. Thousands of copies of the calendar were printed and distributed free each December. The response was excellent, and more and more organizations requested listings.

When the city manager informed all departments that all projects needed to become self-financing, Rita's department head,

Kerwin, ordered that the calendars be sold instead of given away. Rita suspected that few people would actually purchase the calendars. She diligently researched the situation through local bookstores and discovered that it was unlikely that more than a few hundred city calendars could actually be sold. Rita tried to explain her conclusions to Kerwin politely. The city calendar, attractive as a giveaway, would not be able to compete with the many commercially available calendars.

Kerwin, a former military officer, overrode her every objection. When she presented facts and figures to support her initial assessment and asked for direction, Kerwin bellowed, "You know what I want you to do!" and stormed out of the room. Shaken, Rita considered resigning. She made one more attempt to save Kerwin from the probable effects of his bad judgment. She gave him a single piece of paper showing projected sales figures and losses. He ignored it. Rita could almost hear him saying "My mind is made up, don't confuse me with information."

Rita followed orders. Twenty-five thousand calendars were printed, three thousand were sold, two thousand were presented to various city employees, and twenty thousand surplus calendars were warehoused. An investigative reporter discovered the situation, and the subsequent scandal embarrassed many people. The city manager finally announced that no further calendars would be produced.

Rita knew that the emperor had no clothes and tried to tell him so, but he would not listen to her. Later she lamented, "I knew better, but I could not get him to listen to me. I brought him the data, but he ignored it. What else could I have done?"

Kerwin did not want to accept any information (someone else's truth) that conflicted with his own beliefs, and he erected a defense system to ensure his own authority. By attacking Rita, he was able to temporarily avoid hearing threatening information. Rita felt powerless to breach his defenses, or even get his attention. He easily dismissed her normally polite and systematic approach, and she did not want to risk her career by stepping outside the chain of command to call the impending disaster to the attention of Kerwin's boss. Although she did tell the truth, she could not figure out a way to do so powerfully enough to make a difference in an unresponsive and unprotected environment.

Although her options were limited, as one's choices often are when dealing with an autocratic boss, Rita later concluded that her own fear had kept her from insisting that Kerwin listen to her. Fear is an enormous barrier to truth-telling. A strong emotional response often blocks thinking (Goleman 1995), and truth-telling in a hostile environment requires both thoughtfulness and caution. It is easier for all but the most determined truth teller to quietly retreat than it is to insist upon being heard.

Why not just give up? Sometimes this is the best choice, but Rita decided that giving up cost her too much. Two years later she was still confused and angry about the incident because she had compromised her own strong ethical position by following orders she was sure would waste resources she was committed to preserving. She did not want to risk paralysis in a similar situation in the future.

Why Some People Just Won't Listen

You probably hold some cherished beliefs about who you are in the world. You may be convinced that you are a great problem solver, a superior supervisor, or a loving parent. If you receive evidence that contradicts your belief, you may immediately examine your own behavior and take action to fix any problems. But if you are like most ordinary people, you will first try to explain the situation in a way that allows you to keep your belief about yourself intact.

You may tell yourself that you just had a bad day, or that someone else failed to supply you with the information you needed to really understand the problem. Then you can hold on to your belief that you are a great problem solver. For instance, you may explain a difficult situation with a child by telling yourself that he or she is just going through a stage. Then you can still consider yourself a loving parent.

Your explanation of the situation may be absolutely correct, and the lapse may be temporary or caused by something beyond your control. If the evidence mounts that there is really something wrong with your problem-solving ability, or your parenting, or your relationship with your staff, then it is to be hoped that you will reevaluate your beliefs about yourself and do something to correct the situation.

On the other hand, you may be one of those people who hold on to negative beliefs about themselves with the same tenacity others have for seeing themselves in a positive light. If you are convinced that everything is your fault, or that you will never get ahead, you probably have a habit of trying to ignore evidence that does not support your negative beliefs about yourself. It is often hard to accept evidence that you are different than you think you are.

Some people are more committed to their beliefs about themselves than others are. Usually your early life experiences influence how you understand your place in the world. The harsher these life experiences were, the more committed you may be to your own explanation of who you are and what role you must take in order to feel accepted. You may believe that you are a hard worker, a leader, a victim, a caretaker, or a tough guy or gal. You may see yourself as the person who is always in the right, a true believer, a rule enforcer, a nice guy or gal, or someone who always follows orders.

It does not matter what role you have chosen. What is really important is whether or not you understand that the role is only a part of who you are. The real you is the deep inner core of yourself, who decided to adopt the role in the first place, and who can give it up when you see that you no longer need it. The more you have your role confused with your identity, the more threatened you will feel by information that contradicts your belief. The more you understand that your role is not you, the easier it will be to accept new information about any situation.

People who resist paying attention to a truth that differs from what they already believe are usually trying to protect themselves. Unfortunately the protective action eventually causes more problems than it solves.

What to Do If Your Truth Is Ignored

If you are faced with a situation like Rita's, where you present your truth but are ignored, and you need to decide what to do about it, explore these suggestions.

1. *Use your emotional reaction as a signal to remind you to take time to think before you choose how you will act.* You probably cannot avoid your emotional reaction to not being listened to. Our brains are programmed to respond to perceived danger. When something happens that reminds you of a situation that seemed painful or dangerous to you in the past, you react. Your instincts tell you to fight, run away, or freeze. You probably already recognize these reactions in yourself, yet you don't scream, run, cry, or hide every time you feel the urge to do so. But there may be times when you absolutely must get away from a situation. Quietly excuse yourself and go to the restroom.

2. *The first thing to think about is whether you really are in danger.* Although Rita felt at the time that Kerwin was completely unreasonable and unapproachable, and that if she failed to obey him he would be impossible to work with in the future, she did not consider other available information. She had seen him angry before (although never at her), and he had later acted as if nothing had happened. If she had taken time to think things through, she might have realized that she was imagining more danger than actually existed.

3. *Imagine being the person who is not willing to hear your truth.* When Rita tried to walk in Kerwin's shoes, she imagined that he was very concerned about following his own orders, and that he was only concerned with producing income to allow the department to continue its work. As a military officer he was accustomed to following and giving orders, but he did not understand participative management practices. Although he was trying to ease up on his employees, he was uneasy about managing women. Rita imagined that Kerwin was barely aware of his impatient response to her.

4. *Design a way to express your truth that will help your truth blocker attain his or her own goals.* Rita could have provided Kerwin with an alternative solution that would have allowed him to save face because it would not have directly opposed his position. For example, accepting the need to have the calendar production costs covered, she could have proposed inviting local businesses to underwrite the expenses through advertising, and still make the calendar available free to the public.

5. *Design a strategy that will get the attention of your truth blocker.* Rita could have met Kerwin's power with her own and refused to allow his bullying tactics to intimidate her, while still supporting his goal. Her original memos to Kerwin provided information and recommendations for him to evaluate. Presenting her evaluation succinctly and emphasizing its importance by taking protective action might have done the trick:

> I STRONGLY RECOMMEND THAT WE DO NOT AT-TEMPT TO SELL THE CALENDARS BECAUSE
>
> A. We will not be able to sell them.
>
> B. We will not recover our costs.
>
> I am placing this memo in my personnel file to record my objection and protect myself in case you proceed against this well-researched advice.

6. *Consider telling your truth to someone else who can listen and take effective action.* You must consider the relative risks no matter what course you take. Is it worth the potential cost? Rita believed that asking Kerwin to arrange a joint conference with his manager was not an option because by breaking the "chain of command" she would have ruined any possible future relationship with Kerwin. Some situations might warrant that kind of risk, but this was not one of them.

7. *Get a second opinion.* Discuss the situation with someone you trust who is not immediately involved. A trusted person with a fresh point of view can help you see alternatives, and can provide support for your taking action that you can live with.

Reference
Goleman, D. *Emotional Intelligence.* New York: Bantam Books, 1995.

2

It's Hard to Tell the Truth When You Would Rather Not Know What It Is

Robert, the owner of a dry cleaning establishment, could not understand why he was losing money in a store that seemed to be doing lots of business. He was reluctant to accept evidence that his store manager was stealing his supplies.

"I had a gut feeling that something was wrong, but I could not prove anything. Angela was being sweet and stabbing me in the back at the same time. I really felt like a fool when I found out what was going on," Robert said as he recalled the unpleasant and costly situation that had almost ruined his twelve-year-old dry cleaning business.

Distracted by his upcoming wedding, Robert had encouraged his store manager, Angela, to assume more and more responsibility. Since she had been employed with him for eight years, the last two of them as store manager, he was pleased when she relieved him of the day-to-day responsibility of ordering supplies and managing the daily bookkeeping. He felt very comfortable about taking a three-week honeymoon and leaving the business in her care.

When he returned, he noticed a puzzling change in her attitude. He accidentally discovered that she was undercutting his authority with employees by telling them that they did not have to follow his instructions. Once he overheard Angela tell an employee, "You don't have to do that. It's a stupid idea." Robert was uncomfortable about that incident, but he never seemed to find an appropriate time to talk with her about it. He told himself that it "really was not important enough to cause an unpleasant confrontation with an important and trusted employee."

Adjusting to married life kept him busier than usual, and he appreciated Angela's willingness to close the store at the end of the day. Although he was a little uneasy about her occasional moodiness, he was reluctant to embarrass her by talking about it. Robert told himself that she was probably just upset about something, and it would pass. He was really grateful to her, after all, for freeing up his time so he could concentrate on his private life for a while. He assured himself that he would be spending more time at the store soon, and things would return to normal.

Whenever Robert was in the store, customers seemed plentiful. Yet Angela told him that she was concerned that the cash was not balancing properly; the receipts and the cash in the drawer seemed to be off by a few dollars several times a week. Robert suggested that they both watch the employees carefully to try to discover what was wrong with the system. Robert also noticed that the supplies were frequently low, and he asked Angela to stay more alert to maintaining the proper reserves.

The slightly uncomfortable situation became unbearable a few months later when Robert's accountant informed him that the once-profitable store was losing money. Shocked and perplexed, Robert decided to refocus on the business, spend time at the store, and bring things under control himself.

He noticed that although the stock of expensive cleaning supplies remained low, large orders for the supplies had been placed regularly in recent weeks. He was concerned that protocols were not being followed, that supplies were being wasted. He prepared a list of his observations to discuss with Angela during a routine performance review. At that meeting Angela appeared angry that her work was being questioned. Her ultimatum was "Give me my raise or I'm leaving."

Robert asked for advice from his colleagues at a business owner's discussion group he attended regularly at the local chamber of commerce. As he described the situation, some of the businesspeople present suggested that Angela might be taking his supplies and reselling them. They advised him not to give her the raise, to accept her resignation and thereby limit his losses. Although he was reluctant to undergo the difficulty of searching for a new manager, Robert decided to follow their advice.

When he arrived back at the store he made another quick survey of the supplies and discovered that a large unopened vat of dry cleaning fluid was missing. Angela apparently saw what Robert was doing. She quietly left the building, taking some of Robert's financial records with her. She never returned. Robert called the police, but they could do nothing. Later he was glad that the complaint was on record, because Angela sued him for unemployment benefits, claiming that she had been fired unjustly. Because Robert had filed a complaint, Angela lost that suit.

It was only after Robert had hired a new manager and everyone at the shop relaxed that he learned that since her departure, Angela had been trying to turn his employees against him. She had been calling them and telling them how incompetent and unfair he was. He remembered his reluctance to discuss with Angela the earlier incident of her badmouthing him, and he kicked himself for basing a business decision on his personal discomfort—instead of his better judgment.

Business profits improved immediately after Angela left. The first month's figures showed a complete reversal of the six-month-long gradual decline in profits. Later Robert and his accountant pieced together other details of the debacle. Cash receipts had been short $10 to $15 per day for months; and about once a week they had been off by as much as $40. Many supplies that had been ordered were missing and unaccounted for. He and the accountant believed that some dry cleaning sales to customers had probably not even been recorded. They assumed that Angela had started stealing gradually and became more bold when she saw that Robert's attention was elsewhere.

Together with the accountant Robert concluded that attempting to take the matter to court would cost more than they would be able to recover. Since business was good and profits were growing, Robert decided that he had paid expensive tuition for an important lesson, and he put the incident behind him. Almost two years later Robert reports, "I am less trusting now. I don't show my manager all of my figures. I make certain to check things periodically, including the ordering and usage of supplies. Now I don't ignore potential trouble because it makes me uncomfortable. Just a few weeks ago, I heard some backtalk from employees, and I called a meeting immediately. I learned what the problem was and corrected it before there was more trouble. The business is doing very well, and I feel confident about my ability to stay in control."

The Traps of Discounting and Denial

If you, like Robert, find it easy to ignore potentially uncomfortable information, you are not alone. Most people learn selective listening as children. It was easy to hear the ice-cream truck several blocks away, but somehow your mother's voice telling you that it was bedtime barely registered. If you want to learn to identify potentially damaging situations quickly, you can learn to look for signals that you are discounting important information. That way you can let yourself know the truth, even if the truth is unpleasant.

Discounting means automatically filtering out certain types of information, because if you had that information, you would experience some kind of discomfort (Weiss and Weiss 1989). By registering the uncomfortable information, you might feel compelled to do something that you would prefer not to do, or you might lose a cherished illusion. If Robert had registered early signs of Angela's duplicity, he would not have felt comfortable leaving her in charge. At that time in his life he definitely preferred to devote time to his personal life instead of worrying about the business. In order to do so he had to maintain the illusion that he could safely leave the business in Angela's care.

It is possible to filter out all of the information about a particular problem by not even noticing that the problem exists. Robert completely failed to notice that more supplies than usual were being ordered, so he could not even consider the possibility that Angela was stealing from him. He only noticed that supplies were low.

You can notice signs that a problem exists but decide that they are insignificant and not worth your attention. Robert took this path when Angela told him that there were problems with the cash receipts. Looking back, he believes that if he had taken those signs seriously and thoroughly investigated the situation himself, the thefts would have stopped immediately.

You can also discount the possibility of solving a problem, even though you consider the matter important. Robert "could not" figure out a suitable way to confront his trusted manager about her telling an employee to ignore his directions. He knew it was an important problem, but it seemed unsolvable at the time.

It is also common to know that a problem exists, to know that it is important, and to know that it can be solved, but to discount your own or someone else's ability to solve it. Robert did not want to upset Angela by talking about her moodiness, and thus he missed the opportunity to learn more about the situation. Procrastination and excuses such as "too busy," "too tired," "too poor," "too dumb," "too important," "too stressed," or "too uncomfortable" may be clues that you're discounting your own ability to solve a problem. You may filter out information that would allow you to address a problem, because you don't want to spend the time, money, or resources required to solve it.

Selective attention, discounting, or denial (another term to describe the thought process when addictive behavior is involved) are all automatic reactions. They are habits of thought we learned when we were children in order to make our lives more comfortable, because it is often easier to ignore an uncomfortable truth than it is to address it. Yet just because you do this does not mean that you are sick, bad, stupid, or crazy; it just means that you are not paying attention.

Fortunately, *habits can be changed*. If you suspect that you have a habit of not telling yourself the truth because you would rather not know what it is, you can create a new habit that will serve you better. You do not have to wait until a near disaster, like Robert's, demands your attention. You can learn to notice your own self-defeating tendencies, your blind spots.

By reducing the size of your blind spots you increase your flexibility in making moment-to-moment decisions that ultimately affect every area of your life. When you commit yourself to this process, you join the community of truth tellers who are constantly discovering resources and power to dramatically improve many situations.

Changing Your Own Self-Defeating Patterns

Caution! Any process of becoming more aware of yourself takes time. Since you developed your habits for reasons that once made perfectly good sense to you, changing them is a decision only you can make. Sometimes becoming aware of hidden truths is a joyful, refreshing process that allows you to take new risks and proceed in new directions, but sometimes the process is painful and frightening. Avoid self-criticism and congratulate yourself for every bit of progress you make.

1. Start by simply noticing your own internal conversations. When you tell yourself that you should do something, or that you should stop doing something, and then ignore your own advice, STOP!

2. Ask yourself why you are giving yourself the advice, and why you are ignoring it. Just listen to yourself think.

3. Observe the process and notice if it is a sign that you are selectively ignoring information that might be important to you.

4. Decide how you want to use the information you have just discovered.

5. Use the impulse to engage in a habit you would like to change as a signal that tells you that you are probably discounting something.

    a. Each time you have an impulse to reach for a cigarette, eat when you are not hungry, drink another cup of coffee, or automatically turn on the TV, STOP!

b. Reflect on whether there is something you do not want to feel or think about right now, or if there is something else you really need or want. You will probably notice that your habit helps you to distract your attention from something important you need to be seeing about yourself or others, or your situation.

c. Decide what if anything you will do with the information you have discovered, and when you will take action, if you choose to do so.

d. Decide whether or not to eat, have the cigarette, watch TV, and so forth.

6. Congratulate yourself.

Reference

Weiss, L., and J. Weiss. *Recovery from Co-Dependency: It's Never Too Late to Reclaim Your Childhood.* Deerfield Beach, Fla.: Health Communications, 1989.

CHAPTER

3

It's Hard to Tell the Truth
When the Truth Is Bad News

Jennifer is still furious about being squeezed out of her company by being demoted three times. She felt humiliated until she recognized that the same steps had been used to cause others to resign as the company downsized. The people who resigned lost their chance to collect severance pay and other benefits. She refused to be intimidated and left with her dignity and her benefits intact.

Although Jennifer had known for some time that her company was selling off divisions in an attempt to adjust to a rapidly changing environment, she felt relatively secure in her middle management position. As she advanced from production planner in a textile manufacturing plant that employed five hundred workers to the same position in a larger plant, she was grateful that her division was being retained.

When overseas competition and changing customer demands squeezed the company still further, management shifted people and responsibilities around in an attempt to remain competitive. Some people were fired, but Jennifer was among those who were retained and given additional work. Jennifer reflected, "They tried to keep the knowledge people, the workhorses (like me), who could get the job done quickly—even when it meant ruffling someone's feathers."

Perhaps inevitably, Jennifer's production facility was moved from the northeast to the southern United States, and Jennifer's position was moved along with it and given to "someone who would work for half my salary." After six years in a management position, Jennifer accepted a position with greatly diminished responsibilities—as sales assistant to a vice president. Although she retained her former salary and benefits, she found herself taking messages, writing orders, and doing customer research for the vice president, three sales managers, and nine salespeople.

"I kept dropping down in the scheme of things. When they cut back on the sales force, they gave me sales responsibilities, too," Jennifer remembered. "*They (company executives) never told any of us what was happening.* Finally an executive called a meeting of administrative assistants and invited us to resign. The package they offered was almost laughable, and only one person accepted."

Jennifer then spent six unsatisfactory months as an administrative assistant in another division of the company, still receiving the same production planner salary. Finally, after eleven years with the company, she found herself in the embarrassing position of being shown her new duties (how to deliver the mail, clean the coffeepot, and answer the switchboard) by the office manager of her original division. She felt demoralized, but she tried to focus on the positive. "At least I was still working," she told herself.

When Jennifer was demoted this time, she finally realized the secret the company was not sharing. The company executives did not want to fire her or anyone else, because then they would be forced to pay unemployment compensation. So they were trying to make her life so unpleasant that she would resign. The more she thought about it, the more certain she was. Her situation was very similar to that of the other former company employees just before they had actually resigned.

Jennifer remembered the sales manager who never returned from maternity leave. She had intended to return, but when her supervisor told her that she would no longer have an office and would be doing clerical work, she resigned. Jennifer remembered her own boss who finally resigned after his repeated routine requests to attend corporate training programs were turned down. He tried to stay but gave up when his boss stopped returning his phone calls and treated him as if he didn't exist. The same circumstances were played out time and time again. Employees simply gave up and left without their unemployment compensation package.

Knowing that she was not alone and that the demotions had nothing to do with her competency helped Jennifer cope. She decided that management would not get what they wanted from her! She would not give in, and the only way she would leave was if they actually terminated her employment. She was determined to get the benefits she deserved.

During her final months on the job, Jennifer tried to ignore the demoralization she felt. But she noticed that she got sick more often and did not care nearly as much about being responsible at work. Jennifer's three-year ordeal ended when she was finally given six weeks' notice of termination.

Although she knew it was coming and had planned for it, she was still angry about the embarrassment she had suffered because of the underhanded policies of senior management. At the same time she also felt that she had won a battle and left the company with her dignity intact. Because of special conditions, she received six months' severance pay, a year and a half of unemployment benefits, and a year and a half of insurance benefits. This package, combined with a small inheritance, allowed her to move to another state and start her own business.

Was it worth it? Almost two years later Jennifer, now fifty-one, says that she wishes that the company could have been more honest. "The executives would never admit to anything. If they had told us, 'This is the long-term plan, and this is the short-term plan, and this is how you fit in,' then we all would have retained our dignity. It would have been less of an embarrassing ordeal if we all knew what was happening, instead of being forced to function in such a distasteful and insidious atmosphere."

Why Withhold Bad News?

We can only speculate about why this company withheld the bad news from its employees. Perhaps it was because upper management remained in the dark as well. Sometimes everyone hopes for the best and does not want to admit the unthinkable, hoping that something will magically change. Perhaps management was operating on the misguided belief that by keeping the bad news from the employees, the employees would remain confident and continue to do their jobs effectively. If this was the objective, it really backfired. Perhaps the real situation was what Jennifer finally perceived it to be—that in an effort to save money, the company systematically created the embarrassing conditions that forced many employees to resign without claiming the benefits that were due them.

In any case, management's failure to tell the truth created a situation that caused intense and painful negative experiences for all involved. When someone knows a painful situation is inevitable, it is usually easier to address it quickly rather than draw out the discomfort. It is like getting a Band-Aid off quickly to avoid the prolonged discomfort of pulling one hair at a time as it comes off slowly. But if you are not sure that the situation *really is inevitable*, or if you keep hoping it will improve, then you may be hiding the truth from yourself as well as others.

When the truth is bad news, it is not only hard to tell it, it is often hard to recognize and acknowledge it to yourself. This is especially true when everyone around you is also pretending that the painful or difficult situation does not really exist. When the emperor paraded through the town wearing his nonexistent new clothes, only the child's innocent perceptions could clearly penetrate the layers of deception. Everyone else was confused. They were trapped between the evidence of their eyes and the lies they had been told that made them mistrust their own perceptions. They also feared the social consequences of revealing that they saw something different from what their peers saw. These uncertainties and pressures kept them silent and perpetuated the lie.

Jennifer and her coworkers were trapped in a similar web of deception. Since upper management was silent, the employees' personal observations and predictions were not affirmed. In the face of a crumpling organization they each hoped: "If I don't break the spell by talking about what I observe and feel, then I will be safe." *The truth—that the organization was in serious trouble and no one was safe—was much too painful to bear.* This kind of truth shakes everyone to the core of their being. Safety and security (Maslow 1943) are fundamental human needs, and we would rather cling to the illusion that they exist than face the terror of knowing that we are exposed and vulnerable.

Coping with Bad News

When Jennifer acknowledged her true situation and gave up her crumbling illusion of security—"at least she still had a job"—she felt more powerful. Then she had two choices: She could resign with minimal benefits, or she could endure the outward humiliation of demotion and wait until the company took the responsibility for ending her employment. Her choice to hang on long enough to get the benefits she had earned gave her a sense that she retained some of the dignity that was threatened when she felt totally powerless to affect her own destiny.

There are times when you can't change external events. You respond in your own individual and unique way in those situations. Your way depends upon your own life history and your past experiences of your own competency in the face of crisis. Although best-selling author Tom Peters (1987) says that learning to love chaos is necessary to thrive in the current business environment, only a few people are able to follow his advice. If you are one of the fortunate few who learned that your own actions could affect difficult situations, you may be one who thrives on chaos. If you are, then you probably relish the opportunity to grasp the truth, even if it is uncomfortable, so that you can respond quickly and take advantage of new opportunities.

If you belong to the great majority of folks who prefer stability, because you did not have opportunities to successfully manage change in the past, you are vulnerable to self-deception when the truth is not immediately clear or obvious. If you want the advantages that come with clear vision, you must also accept the discomfort of knowing your own vulnerability.

Sometimes the sensation of adrenaline release that comes with the recognition of danger is labeled terror; at other times it is called exhilaration. Your personal label is influenced by your own personality and your earlier life experiences. Some people hate the sensation; others crave it. If you hate it, you may never learn to love it, but you *can* learn to accept it. You can learn to use the adrenaline rush as a signal, to remind you to evaluate whether or not you are in danger. Once you assess any actual danger, you can decide upon an appropriate response.

When you are stuck in a situation that you cannot change and that you do not fully understand, your only true power may lie in your ability to think for yourself. If you suspect that you are being given misinformation or being only partially informed about a situation that affects you, think carefully about what is happening. Consider alternative explanations for the information you are given. Your ability to evaluate your observations can help you protect yourself.

One way to approach a confusing situation is to learn to separate your observations—what you see, hear, feel, taste, and smell— from the conclusions you reach based on your observations *as well as your previous life experiences.* Different people reach different conclusions in similar situations because they interpret the information differently. You will need to deliberately practice this approach until using it becomes a habit.

How You Can Untangle Confusing Situations

1.   Practice approaching situations from the perspective of a videotape recorder. Notice what is actually there to record—the expression on someone's face, the furniture in the room, the relative placement of people, the sound of a voice, the actual words that are being spoken, whether questions are answered or avoided, and so forth. For example, rather than concluding, "He is angry," note, "He is waving his arms in the air, yelling loudly, and his face is red."

2.   Write a description of your observations—just the facts, please. Would another observer be able to see and hear what you

have noted if that person watched the same video? Could you show someone else the details you have noticed? Writing has the advantage of creating an accurate record of your passing thoughts. It is all too easy to lose information that is uncomfortable to think about. If you hate writing, just think through the details of your observations or tell them to someone else.

3.   Now write down your conclusions about the facts you have been observing. Sometimes these conclusions seem very obvious, and sometimes your ideas will seem exaggerated and unreasonable to you. Write your own conclusions about your observations, even if you are uncertain about them.

4.   After you have written down your own conclusions, think of at least three other possible explanations for your observations. Record these, too. It is sometimes useful to include silly or extreme possibilities here, just to stretch your thinking.

5.   Rank all the possibilities according to how accurate you believe they are.

6.   Find someone you trust to help you do a reality check on your observations and conclusions. Share all of your thoughts and ask for further ideas on the subject. The more frequently you practice talking about your perceptions, the easier it will become to either talk about them or act on them in the future.

7.   Keep practicing this process in different situations until you can comfortably see any situation from many different perspectives. This will increase your ability to recognize the truth in situations that may be uncomfortable or threatening.

References

Maslow, A. H. *Motivation and Personality*. New York: Harper & Row, 1970.

Peters, T. J. *Thriving on Chaos: Handbook for a Management Revolution*. New York: Knopf, 1987.

CHAPTER

4

When Truths Collide

*Carol believed her secretary's work should meet certain stan-
dards and told her so. Her secretary, a member of a minority
group, told others that Carol was a "bitch" and threatened to
file a discrimination suit. The harder Carol tried to be nice, the
worse the situation became.*

When Carol had accepted a newly hired minority worker as her
secretary, she had been pleased that her department was actually
meeting its affirmative action goals. She regretted losing the wonderful woman who had been working with her so well for the past
three years, but she expected that breaking in someone new would
be fairly routine. Over the years, Carol had created excellent working relationships with most of her support staff and others she
supervised both by acknowledging their successes and by calmly
asking them to redo any work that did not meet her high standards.

Carol's usual tactics did not seem to work well with Josephine, her new secretary. The first time Josephine gave her a report containing many misspellings, Carol made certain that Josephine was aware of how to use the Spell Check feature on the computer, and asked Josephine to run the Spell Check on the report file and reprint it. Two days later, Carol received the report with most of the errors corrected. She told Josephine that she needed work back more quickly and returned the report for further corrections. A week after Josephine had completed the first version of the original report and given it to Carol, Carol reluctantly accepted the still marginal work from Josephine.

This scenario was replayed with variations for several weeks. Josephine seemingly refused to use the Spell Checker until Carol sent the work back for correction.

Josephine's behavior also invited Carol to discipline her in other areas. Carol repeatedly asked Josephine to stop making long personal calls from her desk during the workday. She asked Josephine to do her work instead of polishing her nails. Several people in the organization told Carol that Josephine was complaining in the cafeteria that Carol was a "bitch." Carol began to feel desperate. She even lost sleep over the situation.

As Carol grew increasingly frustrated, she tried every management technique she could think of to get Josephine to perform more satisfactorily. After five weeks of tearing her hair, Carol told Josephine that her work was unacceptable, and if her work did not improve she would be let go when her three-month probationary period was completed.

Josephine responded angrily that Carol had been out to get her from the beginning, and that if Carol attempted to fire her, she would bring a discrimination suit against the company. Carol informed her own manager, Harold, of the situation, and he decided to observe Josephine's work directly. He "borrowed" Josephine for a few days, and Josephine did adequate work for him. He saw no evidence of the work problems that Carol had been struggling with.

After Josephine returned to Carol, the old problems reappeared by the end of the week. Carol tried every way she could think of to encourage Josephine to do an adequate job. Harold tried to help, but each time Carol did as he suggested, Josephine seemed to get even more angry and resistant. Yet whenever Harold was in the vicinity, Josephine appeared pleasant and cooperative.

At the end of three months, Carol asked Harold to approve of dismissing Josephine. Instead of approving, he suggested an additional three-month probationary period. Carol argued but finally agreed. Because of the threat of a discrimination suit, they would bend over backward to make sure that Josephine would be given every opportunity to succeed. Carol continued to politely request that Josephine do her assigned work, and Josephine continued to be sullen and uncooperative.

After three more months of continuous friction, Josephine was transferred to another department instead of being terminated. Her new supervisor, Ann, gave Josephine very clear descriptions of each task she would need to master in order to remain in her new position. After two more months, Ann said, "Josephine, there are ten things you must be able to do to keep this job, so far you have learned only two of them. I suggest you start looking for another job." After another month, Josephine's employment with the company was terminated.

What Is the Truth?

What individuals believe is true depends on what information they choose to pay attention to. Their perceptions are affected by their values, their past experiences, and their beliefs about themselves, others, and the world in general. Carol, Josephine, Harold, and Ann all experienced their own versions of the truth in this situation.

Carol's experience of the truth was that Josephine was not performing the job adequately. Carol valued respect for all individuals and producing high-quality work. This was the main focus of her attention. Carol believed that she was a nice person and a competent manager, and she felt angry and frustrated when Josephine was unresponsive to her management style and treated her disrespectfully.

Josephine believed that she had a right to do as she pleased in any situation. She strongly valued her own independence and autonomy. She felt angry at Carol for correcting her, and she believed that any woman who told her what to do was a mean bitch. She also believed that when she felt angry, the best thing to do was to retaliate.

Harold's view of the truth was that he was doing the right thing. He valued being fair to minorities. Being fair meant bending the rules, so that minorities would have every opportunity to succeed. He believed that Carol's standards were unnecessarily high.

Ann valued objective measurements and effectiveness. To Ann, the only relevant truth was whether or not an employee could meet objective job standards. Josephine did not meet those standards.

Understanding What Happens When Truths Collide

When people perceive the truth of a situation differently but think they are experiencing things the same way, the results can be confusing. Emotions are an important and relevant component of perceptions about any confused and stressful situation.

Carol and Josephine were both experiencing strong emotional reactions to each other. Carol tried to ignore her emotions and proceed rationally according to her belief about what steps are required to be a good manager. Josephine used her emotions as the launching pad for her actions, without thinking about her emotions or considering the consequences of her behavior. It did not occur to either woman to speak about what she was experiencing emotionally. They were both following a common unspoken rule that emotions are a taboo subject in the workplace. This was unfortunate. Emotions provide important information about what we like, dislike, need, and want, and they can be valuable if you know how to use them effectively.

Emotions are first experienced as internal sensations that arise in response to the pleasures and frustrations we experience in a given situation. As children we learn to interpret these sensations and attach meaning to them. Some people become highly skilled in interpreting these sensations and use them to guide their actions. Others learn to ignore these sensations or pretend that they do not exist. Some emotions have come to be valued as good and others reviled as bad. A more useful understanding is that emotions are simply information about how we are responding to what we are experiencing (Weiss and Weiss 1989; Weiss 1991).

Carol told Josephine the truth about the acceptability of her work. If Carol had told the truth about her emotional reaction to Josephine's inability or refusal to follow directions, perhaps something would have changed. Talking about an emotion does not mean expressing the emotion in an uncontrolled manner. Instead of trying to remain calm or getting overtly angry, Carol might have said, "I feel really frustrated when I have to tell you the same thing over and over again. I think that you are capable of doing this job correctly. What is going on?"

Talking about the content of a situation sometimes becomes a repetitive and unproductive process; people repeat their words or their behavior in an effort to be understood. Since the repetition does not introduce any new information, everyone involved tends to become more frustrated and unhappy. Carol and Josephine's repetitious conversations about the Spell Checker could not change anything, because an important part of what was true for each of them was being omitted from their conversations. When the process of working out a problem gets stuck, a discussion of what is going on between the people involved can lead to new progress.

To change anything, a new conversation—about how the old conversation is stuck—needs to occur. As soon as Carol recognized Josephine's pattern of not using the Spell Check function, Carol could have pointed it out: "Josephine, I have noticed that you do not use the Spell Checker until after I ask you to redo your work." The conversation could then have been about what to do about the pattern instead of about the unsatisfactory work.

Dr. Eric Berne described many of these unproductive, repetitive patterns and labeled them "games" in his best-selling book, *Games People Play* (1964). Games frequently occur in work, as well as in personal relationships. Most people do not consciously notice that they are engaged in a game until it ends, and they experience a familiar, often unpleasant emotion. Often a small rueful voice then whispers, "I should have known that was going to happen." Playing games provides hidden social and emotional advantages to the people who engage in them. Often the game helps confirm deeply held beliefs, such as "If you want something done right, you have to do it yourself," or "People always take advantage of me." We respond to opportunities to prove these beliefs to ourselves by inviting others (who need to reinforce their own beliefs about themselves and the world) to play games with us.

Josephine would invite supervisors to correct her in order to "prove" to herself that she was being victimized by mean people. Carol's repeated corrections gave Josephine lots of opportunities to experience herself as a victim. Ann declined Josephine's invitation to play the game by refusing to discuss Josephine's inadequate work and simply delivering appropriate consequences.

Whenever game playing occurs, people act out the roles of Persecutor, Rescuer, and Victim in relationship to each other (Karpman 1968). They tend to switch roles frequently. First Josephine feels like a victim of persecutor Carol, but soon Carol feels like a victim of persecutor Josephine. Carol sometimes tries to help and rescue Josephine—but then she becomes a victim of Josephine. Truth-telling becomes a casualty in this repetitive process.

Noticing the game or the experience of feeling like a persecutor, an ineffective rescuer, or a victim can become the signal that an important truth is hidden and needs to be addressed. A simple way to be open to receiving this truth is to say to yourself, "I'm not sure just what is happening, but if we continue this we will soon be arguing [be stuck, be angry, and so forth] just like we were before." Then try to learn the missing truth by asking yourself what you think each game player is trying to accomplish in the interaction. Once you have identified that the game is being played, you will be in a position to stop playing your contributing role and to help put an end to the game.

What You Can Do When You Suspect Someone Is Playing a Game

1. Notice your own emotions. Pay attention to the physical sensations you are experiencing as you encounter various situations. These sensations can give you important information

about your own subtle perceptions, which you may not be able to describe with words.

2.   Describe your emotional response to yourself. Use this simplified list to help label your feelings: sad, mad, glad, scared, or ashamed. Most complex emotions involve a combination of these basic feelings (Weiss and Weiss 1989; Weiss 1991).

3.   Notice whether you feel like a Persecutor, a Rescuer, or a Victim in the game. You may start out in one position, move through other positions, and then end up in any position when the process ends.

4.   Ask yourself what you are trying to accomplish in your interaction with the other person. Look for the hidden truth behind the obvious truth. For example, many people tell themselves they are just trying to be heard (the obvious truth), when the truth is that they are really trying to be liked (the hidden truth).

5.   Once you understand your hidden agenda, think of a simple, direct way that you can accomplish your objective. (You might decide that your hidden objective is inappropriate in your current situation. If that is the case, think about finding a new situation where you can achieve your goal. For example, you may never get the approval you seek from your supervisor, but you might be able to get it from a friend.)

6.   When you are stuck in a repetitive process with someone, one possible approach is to tell that person about the feeling(s) you are experiencing. Simply describe the feelings. Attempt to stay calm; instead of sounding angry or scared, simply talk about the feeling. You might say, "I have noticed that whenever we talk about this, I feel like yelling. I won't yell, but I think I am feeling really angry about this situation."

7.   Another approach is to describe the repetitive process you have observed or that you feel you are caught up in. You could describe a series of events or steps that you have noticed coming into play. Use the form, "First I did this . . . then you did that. Next I did this . . . then you responded this way." And so forth. Speak calmly and nonjudgmentally in order to not threaten or alienate the other person.

8.   Decide the next action you need to take to accomplish your objective, and take it.

References

Berne, E. *Games People Play.* New York: Grove Press, 1964.

Karpman, S. B. "Script Drama Analysis." *Transactional Analysis Bulletin* 1968, 7(26): 39–43.

Weiss, L. *I Don't Need Therapy, But . . . Where Do I Turn for Answers?* Deerfield Beach, Fla.: Health Communications, 1991.

Weiss, L., and J. Weiss. *Recovery from Co-Dependency: It's Never Too Late to Reclaim Your Childhood.* Deerfield Beach, Fla.: Health Communications, 1989.

CHAPTER
5

I Want to Be a Team Player, so I Won't Make Waves

Fred did not want to think about the financial status of his company. His management team obliged him by not troubling him with the negative information they had accumulated. His belief in his own invulnerability almost cost him his company.

When Fred's best customer noticed signs of financial problems and asked Fred whether he was about to declare bankruptcy, Fred finally decided to examine the financial records of his seventeen-year-old construction company. After searching through stacks of records, he estimated that he was almost $100,000 short of what he needed to keep the company running for the next month. He could not really be sure because he had never been very interested in understanding his bookkeeper's record-keeping systems. Arthur, his bookkeeper and comptroller, had always managed to provide the data that the CPA required for preparing taxes, and that was good enough for Fred. Fred knew that the company had come through many shaky times, but things had always managed to turn out all right.

This time Fred was worried enough to call a consultant, Diane, who had been helping create job descriptions and an operations manual for Fred's twenty-five-person company. Diane asked that the accountant provide financial statements for the past three years, but Arthur was able to supply data for only the past two and a half years. Arthur explained, "Fred fired the accountant who issued the monthly statements and reviews of the company's status, because he did not think they were necessary." As a result there were no statements for the preceding nine months, and the previous year's books had not been closed.

As Diane tried to understand the situation, she learned that signs of financial trouble had existed for months. The company's $150,000 line of credit had been fully extended for six months, and rushing to find the money to meet the payroll had become normal. Credit at the local building supplier, where bills needed to be cleared monthly, had also been frequently closed down. Even the receptionist had noticed the increased number of calls from vendors requesting payments.

The management team—Fred; Fred's wife, Wendy; Arthur and Lois, the general manager of the residential division—all knew about the ongoing problems. But everyone wanted to be a team player, and nobody felt it was his or her place to insist that Fred or anyone else look at the overall picture. It took the concern of an outsider, Alex, to blow the whistle.

Alex had overseen the construction of many supermarkets and had used Fred's company to build four of them. Now he was hearing disturbing reports from subcontractors that Fred's company was not paying them. On the previous projects Fred had paid subcontractors promptly. Alex knew the warning signs of a contractor in trouble. Another contractor had created a huge headache for him by declaring bankruptcy before a project was complete, and Alex did not want to repeat the experience. When Alex confronted Fred, Fred had to stop ignoring the incipient disaster.

As Diane sifted through the bits and pieces of financial information, she discovered a problem that everyone knew about but no one was willing to talk about. Wendy, who had joined the business four years before, had been developing a business of her own for almost a year, an exclusive women's apparel shop. The new venture had been occupying most of her time, and she had been financing the startup costs with cash loans from Fred's company. Each time she needed another $10,000 she asked Arthur whether the company had the cash to loan her, and each time he said yes. Everyone, including Arthur and Wendy, was shocked to learn that the loans totaled $230,000. Arthur was aware that this large outlay was creating a drain on the company, but he did not want to upset anyone by mentioning it. He assumed that if Fred wanted to discuss the situation, Fred would bring it up.

Meanwhile Wendy had also added several family members to the company payroll. Some made a real contribution to the company, but others received full pay for part-time work.

Lois, general manager of the residential division, was aware that some of her division's workers had been used to construct Wendy's apparel shop and that Wendy had not been charged for the materials or labor. It was part of Lois's job to carefully coordinate materials purchases in order to not be caught short when credit was cut off toward the middle of each month. Yet she, too, said nothing to Fred or anyone else about how Wendy's new business was affecting the construction company's finances. She "did not want to cause trouble." She later told Diane, "You know that something is wrong when you see all this money leaving a company."

With the help of the company's CPA, Diane discovered that the company was short $250,000. The CPA confided that Fred had ignored his repeated warnings that the company needed better financial control procedures. Fred admitted to Diane that he enjoyed managing building projects much more than he enjoyed managing the company. He was operating from a strong belief that things would work out, and he let members of his management team use their best judgment in each situation. They all wanted to please him. Since telling him the truth did not please him, they did not consider truth-telling to be an important part of their job descriptions.

Everyone had wanted to support Wendy in her new endeavor, so nobody asked too many questions about letting her use the construction company to support her new business. After all, she was Fred's wife, and he was not opposing her.

In the end, Diane advised Fred to hire an experienced comptroller and turnaround manager to get the company back on course. Once they took the necessary actions, they managed to save the company from filing bankruptcy. Today Fred is drawing half his former salary. Lois refused to accept a salary cut and left the company. Arthur is operating as a bookkeeper under the supervision of the new comptroller. Wendy admitted she was having an affair with the manufacturer's representative of one of her chief suppliers, and she filed for a divorce. She was officially fired from the company after she failed to show up for work for three months.

This really did happen. Identifying details have been changed to protect everyone involved.

Groupthink

Sometimes members of a team withhold or invalidate their own perceptions because they fear that speaking up will be an unwelcome challenge to the most fundamental beliefs of the group. As a result the decisions made by the team may be even less effective than those made by individual members of the team. Groupthink is a process wherein illusions of invulnerability and unanimity lead individuals to suppress their own doubts rather than risk antagonizing the leader or other members of the team. When no team member is willing to risk social disapproval within the group by revealing his or her view of the truth, the stage is set for disastrous decisions. President John F. Kennedy learned this lesson after examining the decision-making process that led to the Bay of Pigs debacle. In a classic well-researched book, *Victims of Groupthink*, Irving L. Janis (1972) examined the decision-making process that led to this famous embarrassment of the Kennedy administration. Fred's company was also a victim of groupthink. Although Kennedy's process took place around a conference table at the highest levels of government and Fred's in a small business with informal meetings, the same principles were operating in both cases.

Everyone shared Fred's illusion of invulnerability. Things had always worked out in the past, even when times were tough. Why should this time be any different? Since the company's decision makers had already decided to support Wendy in developing her store, why should anyone question anything? The decision had already been made. Even though both Arthur and Lois devoted a lot of time to dealing with the problems caused by lack of cash, they were reluctant to examine the overall financial picture, because then they might have to challenge the decision to fund Wendy's new business. So the evidence that the company was in trouble was minimized. Management meetings focused on crisis management instead of the reason for the crisis.

Fred even protected the status quo by insulating the group from the influence of outside experts, another characteristic of Groupthink. He refused to heed the advice of his CPA to use better control procedures. Then he had dismissed the accountant who was pulling together the monthly figures that would have revealed the growing financial crisis.

On some level, Fred must have sensed the breakdown of his twenty-year marriage to Wendy. To avoid facing this painful truth—which would have been evident had he really examined all the aspects of the situation—he found reasons to focus his attention elsewhere. His management team helped him avoid the truth about the company's predicament until evidence from outside the business forced him to acknowledge what was going on.

Groupthink is a collaborative process. It is a conspiracy of silence designed to protect everyone involved from facing some uncomfortable threat to the integrity of the group. Any group member who calls attention to the shared secret risks either being ostracized from the group or destroying the illusion that the group is a well-functioning team. In this scenario, maintaining the illusion of unity is so important to the emperor's advisors that they ignore the words of the child and play along with the illusion that the emperor's garment really has these fine properties. They go on pretending that they can see the emperor's nonexistent clothing, because acknowledging the truth is too risky. Groupthink is usually revealed only when the negative consequences of faulty decision making finally surface.

The emperor himself (Kennedy or Fred) needs to take a proactive leadership role if he wants to limit further damage and prevent groupthink from occurring in the future (the same advice should be heeded by empresses). If you are in the midst of a dysfunctional situation, you may think that the following steps are overly simple. But remember that the decisions that led to the successful resolution of the Cuban missile crisis were made by Kennedy and the same group of advisors who had just botched the Bay of Pigs situation. The difference was that after advisors discovered the flaws in the earlier decision-making process, Kennedy instituted reforms similar to these.

Preventing Groupthink When You Are the Leader

1. Accept criticism of your judgment. (This will not happen if others are unwilling to risk criticizing you.) You will probably need to start the process by admitting your own mistakes and demonstrating that you are willing to discuss them.

2. Ask each member of your group to act as a critical evaluator of all the information presented to the group. Then make space at each meeting for members to share their thinking. Focus the criticism on what the information implies rather than on the people who are presenting it.

3. Acknowledge the fact that group members are making contributions and thank them, even if you do not agree with the ideas or information they present.

4. Withhold your own ideas and preferences until the discussion is well under way so that group members do not immediately adopt your ideas without considering their own alternatives.

5. Encourage discussion of all ideas and options, especially those that you disagree with. Search for alternative courses of action.

6. Reexamine the positive and negative consequences of all major alternatives before making a final choice or decision.

7. After the decision has been made and implemented, your job is NOT done. Encourage your team to keep evaluating the

results. Be prepared to abandon your decision and repeat the decision-making process if necessary.

8. Use this process to learn to continuously challenge your own assumptions.

Preventing Groupthink When You Are a Member of the Team

Learn to tell your own truth with grace and skill. Part Two of this book discusses a variety of skills that will help you do this.

Reference

Janis, I. L. *Victims of Groupthink*. Boston: Houghton Mifflin, 1972.

CHAPTER

6

I Would Be Glad to Tell the Truth If Only I Knew What It Was

Ron was not really aware of the resentment he felt toward his wife, who was also his business partner. He could not tell her the truth, because he had never noticed his own feelings. Instead, he acted out his anger by not keeping agreements he made with her.

Doris and Ron were concerned that the tensions created between them by their three-year-old catering business were going to destroy either the business, their marriage, or both. Doris had started the business, without much planning, by offering to help several friends manage their large parties. Within six months she was so busy that she and Ron decided to create a real business together.

She resigned from her job so that she could spend all her time developing the business, and he spent evenings and weekends working with her. The business grew rapidly. When Ron's company downsized nine months later, he accepted an early retirement package and joined her full-time in "their" business. They worked out what seemed to be a reasonable plan to share company responsibilities, and they held weekly planning meetings to update each other on results.

Doris had many ideas about growing the company, and Ron usually agreed to implement her ideas. Occasionally, and then more and more frequently, he would not find time to keep his commitments. Doris found his explanations plausible, but as the scenario repeated itself, she began to feel frustrated, and got into the habit of questioning him about the progress of his work. He would angrily accuse her of nagging, and she would counter by accusing him of not caring about the business. As this argument was repeated, with variations, time and again, the situation deteriorated.

In desperation they consulted a counselor, who observed their struggle and helped them understand that their constant arguments were the *symptoms*, rather than the *cause* of their problems. When the counselor asked Ron to explain his thought process when he was making agreements that he did not honor, a pattern emerged.

Instead of feeling like a partner in the business, Ron felt like a slave. Each time Doris had another new idea, he found himself torn between supporting her and doing his own work. He wanted to grow the business, but he felt overwhelmed by the volume of work he was already committed to doing. He did not tell his wife the truth about his growing desperation because he believed that she would be angry if he refused to help her implement her ideas. At the same time Ron recognized the real value of many of Doris' ideas and felt that he ought to carry them out, so he kept on agreeing to take on more work.

Although Ron was not aware of it, he was actually angry at Doris for not understanding that she was contributing to the problem. Her barrage of creative ideas for the business kept him so busy that he could not pursue his own direction or complete anything he started. He was not really aware of feeling angry—just a little frustrated. Certainly not frustrated enough to make an issue of it. He could not tell the truth about his own anger because he was not aware of it. Suppressing the anger drained his energy even more than actually doing the work, so he fell further and further behind.

Doris felt betrayed when Ron failed to keep his commitments. When she tried to protect herself by checking up on him, his hidden anger surfaced, and he turned it on her. The original reason for his anger—her lack of understanding of his situation—remained hidden from both of them.

With the counselor's help, they both finally understood this pattern, and they made some new agreements about how to relate to each other. Ron agreed to voice his ambivalence instead of automatically agreeing to implement Doris's good ideas. Doris realized that she could easily generate enough ideas to keep several people busy. She agreed to ask for his help to evaluate which ones would most benefit the business. Then, together, they would choose which ones Ron would tackle. She also agreed to give him more "air time" in their conversations, rather than filling in any pauses with more good ideas. With practice, and several relapses when they repeated the pattern again, they gradually learned to support each other more appropriately. Two years later, the business and marriage are both thriving.

Passive-Aggressive Behavior Is the Tip of the Iceberg of Hidden Truth

You can feel attacked even when another person has not done anything. In fact, this is the essence of the confusion surrounding passive-aggressive behavior. Passive-aggressive behavior like Ron's is common when individuals make agreements that they are ambivalent about keeping. It is easy to spot this symptom of serious problems: when one person, in this case Ron, is passive about following through on an agreement, the second person, Doris, feels like a victim of angry aggressive behavior. We usually associate the term *aggressive* with an active confrontation of some kind. Instead of openly expressing ambivalence, opposition, or resentment, someone acting in a passive-aggressive manner "attacks" you by not doing what he or she has agreed to do. As a result you feel as surprised, hurt, or angry—as if you have actually been attacked.

This behavior is puzzling to the victim, because the aggressor does not seem to be acting aggressively at all. Take Doris and Ron, for instance. He often sincerely tries to please others by taking on more and more work, trying to do it, and burying his resentful feelings about the stress. At the last minute he apologizes for not managing to complete the assignment, and he implies that the victim should be understanding of the situation. The victim feels anything but charitable, but usually hides the truth about her feelings and tries to be nice about it.

Tension builds until the victim, feeling increasingly frustrated, reaches her limit. When she finally acts to protect herself, usually by trying to be assertive about what she wants, the aggressor then feels "justifiably" angry about being attacked, nagged, and/or not trusted. The ensuing argument then diverts attention away from the original issue of when or whether the task will get done. The secret truth that is rarely revealed is that the aggressor started out feeling angry about real or imagined mistreatment by the victim.

Of course, both men and women can play either role in this frustrating drama. This is another way to understand what is behind the game playing that was described in Chapter 4, and the general directions for avoiding games that we outlined there are useful in a situation like Doris and Ron's.

In this drama, neither the aggressor nor the victim is being truthful. They are both concerned that if they actually tell the truth about how they feel, they will be criticized for having such feelings. Both parties "act nice" when they are angry or scared, trying to do what they think they are supposed to do, until the feelings become too strong to ignore. Then the argument begins, and the pretense that all is well is exposed as false. Yet by that time so many things are wrong that it is difficult to sort out who did what to whom, and it does not really matter anyway. What is important is to focus on what each individual needs and how to solve the problems created by the confusion.

What You Can Do When You Feel Like You Are a Victim of Passive-Aggressive Behavior

1. Notice when you feel angry. Emotions are important signals that can direct you to problems that need attention. Anger usually signals interference with your getting something you

want or need. Angry energy can be transformed to energy for problem solving (Weiss 1991).

2. Ask yourself why you are angry. Knowing the reason for your feeling can seem simple, but it is often complex. You may feel angry at a person, but when you examine your anger in more detail, you may be angry at an inconvenience that person's behavior has caused you. Sometimes you are angry about a pattern of behavior, because of how it effects you.

Ron might not have been angry about any individual thing that Doris asked him to do; but her multiple requests were not allowing him time to complete anything, and that became a real problem. Doris was most angry because of the uncertainty she experienced. She never knew whether or not Ron would keep the agreements he made.

Once you identify the reason for feeling angry, search for the immediate problem that triggered your feeling. If you are the person in Doris's position, you are usually the first one to identify a problem. Often the problem is that someone eise has failed to keep an agreement he or she has made with you. Remember, problem solving involves channeling your angry energy instead of dumping it on anyone else.

3. If someone fails to meet the terms of an agreement, arrange to speak with the person. State your understanding of the agreement. Tell the other person that you are unhappy that the agreement was not kept as you understood it would be.

4. Ask the other person what they understood the original agreement to be. Many agreements are not clearly stated, and each party may understand an agreement differently.

5. Together, clarify what happened and figure out how the misunderstanding occurred.

6. Renegotiate the agreement if necessary, encouraging the other person to make the new agreement only if he or she is willing and able to honor it. This is a very important step. Many people really do want to please others, and they are uncomfortable saying no to any request. You need to make it very clear to the person who has disappointed you that you *are* willing to take no for an answer. Coming to such an understanding is often

the only way to avoid disappointment and frustration in the future.

7.   Make a brief written notation of the new agreement: include specific times and check-in points. Both of you should initial it. This is just to ensure that you are both agreeing to the same thing.

8.   Decide what you will do if this agreement is not honored. Communicate your plan of action to the other person now, instead of waiting to surprise him or her with it after the agreement has been broken. Avoid threats. Make sure that the action you propose is not punitive, and that you will be able to carry out sanctions without causing any damage to yourself. If the agreement is broken, take the action. You may be tempted to allow one more chance, but if you do, you will encourage more passive-aggressive behavior.

9.   If you notice a pattern of broken agreements, try to discover the underlying problem by discussing it instead of pretending that it does not exist. Patterns like this that are ignored tend to get worse with time. Although it may be uncomfortable to address the problem now, you will save yourself future frustration by just facing it.

10.   If you don't have the skill to do this yourself, get help as soon as you can. Passive-aggressive behavior can poison business and personal relationships and does not get better by itself.

What You Can Do If You Get Into Trouble By Saying "Yes" When You Want to Say "No"

1.   Notice when you feel angry.

2.   Identify the reason you feel angry. Read the expanded explanation of both of these points in the "Victim" list that precedes this section.

3.   Learn to recognize the signals that you are feeling overwhelmed. Some people report feeling scared, others tired, and still others feel frenzied. Your own signal is unique to you.

When you detect the signal, it may mean that you are about to cause a problem for yourself and others.

4.   Decide whether or not you will honor your present commitments.

5.   If you can't or won't honor a commitment, tell whoever is involved about the problem right away. Now is the time to renegotiate any agreement that you are not going to keep. It does not matter whether or not you *want* to or *can* keep the agreement—if you are not going to keep it, talk about it.

6.   Make only agreements that you are willing to keep and intend to keep. That means that you need to think about both your feelings and your current situation before you say yes to anything. Sometimes it helps to say, "I need time to think about whether to make this agreement. I will give you an answer by (some specific time)." Then keep the agreement to give the other person your answer.

7.   Learn to say no! Practice helps. Practice saying no or "I don't want to" aloud when you are alone at least twenty times a day for several weeks. Notice how your feelings and energy change as you do this. Then begin to say no to the things you really don't want to do.

8.   Pay attention to your own wishes and dreams. You may be so caught up with whether or not to do what others wish that you have forgotten yourself. Create goals for yourself based on what you want to accomplish.

9.   Cooperate fully when someone invites you to have the kind of conversation that is described in the suggestions for people who feel like victims.

10.   Read a book or take a class about assertiveness training.

Reference

Weiss, L. *I Don't Need Therapy, But . . . Where Do I Turn for Answers?* Deerfield Beach, Fla.: Health Communications, 1991.

CHAPTER

7

Maybe the Emperor Really Is Wearing Clothes, and I Can't See Them

Marilyn, a new technician, thought she saw The Doctor spill a drop of radioactive material on the floor, but she was not quite sure, so she did not speak about it. The radioactive material had indeed spilled, and it took two working days to clean up the contamination in the laboratory. Marilyn did not even share the story until years later.

Marilyn was thrilled with her new job as a technician in a radioisotope research laboratory at a prestigious university hospital. Although she was just out of college and was on the lowest rungs in the lab hierarchy, she loved being around intelligent people who were doing exciting research. She proudly wore the special badge that was inspected weekly to make certain that she was not exposed to too much radioactivity.

She was especially awed by The Doctor, who was the chief researcher as well as a surgeon. He would occasionally move through the laboratory like a whirlwind, wearing his scrubs and giving orders. Sometimes his orders, such as "Take these pieces [tissue samples] of Mrs. Smith . . . ," disconcerted her, but she diligently learned to use the complex equipment, followed the protocols, and learned how to safely handle very low level radioactive materials. She looked forward to learning how to use the remote-control handling equipment behind the thick lead walls of the "cave" that dominated the center of the laboratory.

About two months after Marilyn joined the laboratory staff, a new shipment of extremely radioactive material arrived, and everyone watched as its lead container was safely placed in the cave. As eight people watched respectfully, The Doctor used the remote controls to open the container, dilute a small amount of the material so that it could be used in current experiments, and then reseal the original container.

Marilyn watched intently as The Doctor removed the diluted material from the cave and handed it to another researcher who placed it in a less shielded part of the lab. She thought she observed a drop of the radioactive liquid spilling on the floor during the transfer, but since nobody else said anything, she assumed that she must have been mistaken. So she said nothing.

She forgot the incident until a few days later when a routine monitoring of the laboratory revealed widespread radioactive contamination of many areas of the floor as well as the bottom of people's shoes. The greatest concentration of contamination was traced to the spot just outside the cave where she thought she had seen the droplet spill.

Marilyn maintained her silence, enduring the treatment everyone in the lab was subjected to so that any possible radioactive contamination was quickly removed from their bodies. Work was interrupted for two days as the laboratory was carefully decontaminated. She did not think about the experience again for over thirty years.

I know the intimate details of this story because I was Marilyn. I was twenty-one years old when this incident occurred, and I did not remember it until I started to work on this book. I know that at the time of the incident I was quite certain that The Doctor was infallible, and that my own perception had to be mistaken. After the contamination was discovered, I said nothing about witnessing the spill because I was afraid to admit that I could have prevented a serious problem.

I remember feeling a little bit guilty about not telling the monitoring crew what I knew when they were trying to figure out the cause of the contamination. At that time I believed that telling the truth would have meant accusing The Doctor (the emperor) of having made a mistake. It seemed much smarter to keep my information to myself.

In retrospect, I believe that if I had said something about the spill at the time it occurred, the problem would have been verified and corrected immediately. I also think that if I had waited and only later accused The Doctor of causing the problem, I would have been severely reprimanded for not reporting the problem when I first noticed it. I would have deserved the reprimand; it might have taught me that I was supposed to be a responsible member of the team. Up to that time, however, I had been told to focus only on my own work and ignore everything else.

At age twenty-one I was anxious to please everyone in a position of authority. I even had to lie to myself in order to avoid embarrassing The Doctor. I now wonder if any others in the lab had also seen the spill and pretended not to. Self-deception is easy if telling the truth is not actively encouraged.

Encouraging Responsibility, Initiative, and Truth-Telling

Someone like Marilyn lives in every workplace where supervisors consider themselves too important to establish an atmosphere and an expectation that even the youngest and least experienced workers can make valuable contributions to the good of the team. If I had been instructed to report my observations of anything irregular, I'm sure that I would have dutifully done so. Since I was told to follow exact procedures and never take any initiative, that is exactly what I did.

If my supervisors, the doctor or his assistant, had practiced a few basic people management principles, the outcome might have been quite different. If I had ever been treated as a valuable member of a team, or felt recognized and appreciated, I probably would have trusted both my own perception and the situation enough to call attention to the spill immediately.

Basic Principles of People Management

The first principle is simple. "What you stroke is what you get" is a shorthand way of expressing a basic psychological truth. Behavior to which you pay attention increases. Strokes are the basic recognition we all seek because they fulfill a fundamental human need. When we receive recognition for anything, we are being fed. Sometimes the food tastes good (praise), and we enjoy it; sometimes it tastes bad (criticism), and we hate it. But it nourishes us nevertheless. We tend to repeat behavior that brings us the recognition (food) we need (Berne 1964). Most people will strive for recognition that feels good and avoid negative recognition unless that is the only kind of recognition that is available.

I was stroked very little by my supervisors at the lab. I was told what to do, and I did it. When I completed one assignment, I was given another. I do not recall ever being told that I had done a good job. I do recall a few instances in which I was told about mistakes I had made, but the biggest mistake I made was never alluded to in my presence. I was simply given other responsibilities.

This stroking pattern was and still is standard procedure in many organizations. Good behavior (such as being responsible or telling the truth) is expected yet rarely acknowledged. Undesirable behavior either gets lots of attention because management wants to encourage positive change, or it is not mentioned because of an attitude that implies "Why bother? People are too stupid to change anyway." Of course, that attitude has the unintended result of diminishing good behavior and increasing undesirable behavior. What you stroke *is* what you do get.

My chief rewards at the lab were opportunities to learn new and interesting things as my assignments became more complex. I received most of my personal recognition from other technicians and support personnel—on breaks. Quite naturally, I began to enjoy longer and longer breaks more than my work.

I did not really consider my supervisors to be real people with real interests or goals. I was awed by them but developed no loyalty to them. If I had had a different relationship with them as people, I might have been more able to see myself as a responsible person on the team and would have trusted my own perceptions more.

By not stroking me and doing nothing to support a relationship with me, my supervisors reinforced my belief that I had nothing to contribute except by doing exactly what I was told to do. When I left, they might have wondered why it was difficult to retain employees, or perhaps that idea never occurred to them. As far as I know, they had no awareness or concern about discovering the truth about what employees needed to perform effectively.

The second principle is an extension of the first. "Catch people doing something right!" In the extremely popular *The One Minute Manager*, Ken Blanchard and Spencer Johnson (1982) illustrate this principle. They suggest setting clear goals and recognizing any behavior that shows progress toward those goals.

If my supervisors had watched carefully and stroked behavior that demonstrated responsibility, initiative, thoughtfulness, or truthfulness, I would have developed those traits. Instead I was reprimanded when I suggested a different way of doing things. The message was clear: "Do not think independently. Just focus on doing your job."

I stayed at that job less than a year. When I was offered an opportunity to teach science to young adolescents, I accepted. I thrived on the opportunity to teach creatively and still look back fondly on that career.

If you are supervising entry-level employees and want to help them become responsible members of your team, you need to create an atmosphere that supports their self-esteem and encourages their initiative.

How to Catch People Doing Something Right

1. Clearly define the technical aspects of your employees' jobs, and train them to do those tasks. This step is basic and is usually managed well.

2. Acknowledge your employees as they learn. Stroke them for what they do correctly rather than waiting for them to make a mistake and focusing only on that.

3. Tell them about the broad goals of your organization and how their jobs fit into the big picture. If their job is to fill orders, they need to know that your purpose is to serve your customers well so that they come back and do business with you over and over again. Tell your employees you want all customers to be so pleased with the service they get that they tell their friends about how satisfying it is to do business with your company.

4. Tell your employees about the attitudes you would like them to develop. If you want them to demonstrate responsibility, initiative, thoughtfulness, and/or truthfulness, let them know, even if they do not yet understand exactly what you mean. If you demonstrate these qualities, they will learn by following your example.

5. When you see them demonstrate this positive behavior, stroke it. Tell them you notice and that you appreciate what they are doing. When people are praised for doing something right, two things happen. They feel good, and they repeat the behavior whenever they have an opportunity to do so.

References

Berne, E. *Games People Play*. New York: Grove Press, 1964.

Blanchard, K., and S. Johnson. *The One Minute Manager*. New York: Morrow, 1982.

CHAPTER

8

Facing Ethical Dilemmas

When Allen was given advance notice that the profitable store he managed was going to close, he was ordered to keep it a secret from his loyal customers and his suppliers. He felt trapped between his responsibility to carry out the wishes of his employer and his personal commitment to integrity.

Seven months after Allen assumed management of the second smallest record store in a privately held chain, upper management ordered him to "gut the assets of the branch" and tell the employees that they would soon lose their jobs. Allen was told to inform customers and loyal employees that the owner, Mario, was being forced to take these measures. He was told to say that although money and energy had been invested in the store, the owner could no longer afford to keep it open.

Allen, an experienced manager, was furious. He knew that he had been hired to update and turn around the twelve-year-old store because of his previous success in similar situations. Although he had limited access to the financial data about his store, he was quite certain that his was one of the few in the chain that was making a profit. Allen knew that Mario had not made any recent financial investments in this particular store. "He had not done any marketing in several years," Allen said. In fact, Mario had ignored the older, more established stores as he tried to develop new outlets. In an attempt to cut expenses, Mario had recently merged another store, which had focused on the classical record market, with Allen's store.

With the help of his "trustworthy, knowledgeable, and mature staff," who had from five to over forty years of experience in the record business, Allen had changed the mix of inventory, and as a result sales were brisk. The store was supporting a loyal customer base for both the classical and the popular lines, and it was attracting new shoppers regularly, even though it was located in a marginal shopping area.

Allen believed that Mario had other reasons for closing the store. Maybe he simply wanted to get out of the specialized classical market completely and use the cash invested in the old location to bolster the newer ones. But Allen felt that it was unfair and unnecessary to abandon long-term, loyal employees and customers as long as he could keep his store profitable, and he was certain that he could.

What Allen was most angry about was the deviousness of Mario's instructions. "If Mario had just said, 'I need to free cash from the inventory because I have just opened a hungry larger store' that would have been forthright. I would have fought and said I thought it was counterproductive. But he lied! He wanted me to tell people that he had put resources and experts into my store and the finances still would not work. That simply was not true."

Allen expressed his dilemma to a discussion group on the Internet: "I'm being asked to spin a lie for PR purposes which is the least of it. . . . I feel bifurcated: need the paycheck, don't want to be the hatchet man or liar." His anguish evoked several thoughtful and challenging responses.

Within a few weeks Allen arranged a meeting one-on-one with Mario where, according to Allen, "I completely unloaded my frustrations, but did so in as constructive a manner as possible." The meeting produced mixed results. Mario fired the company's vice president of operations, who had been promoting the strategy of closing the smaller store to support the larger ones. At a chainwide meeting three weeks later, Allen heard information that made him feel even more hopeful. All the managers were promised more financial information and more control over their own profit centers, but this promise was not kept.

Five months after that meeting, Allen's store was still open, and Allen was still waiting for the promised information and control. Finally he concluded that Mario, a fiftyish self-made entrepreneur and first-generation American, did not trust his employees. Allen reported, "I was allowed to make my store profitable, but I still have to guess about the profit/loss situation. I don't have detailed expense information. I don't even know how much is spent on rent. I have made the inventory as attractive as possible, but I have reached the limit of what I can do. I continue to manage the store although my own motivation is minimal."

What Do You Owe an Employer Who Doesn't Support You?

The situation at the record store presents two problems. The first was Allen's dilemma about whether to be loyal to his employer by lying to his staff and his customers. Allen resolved that problem by developing a third option: directly confronting Mario. He showed his loyalty to Mario by offering his evaluation of the situation and making suggestions about alternative methods of handling things.

The second problem was caused by a promise that was not kept. Mario did not even know that this problem existed. Whether or not Mario trusted his managers is unknown. But by not keeping his agreement to share information, despite Allen's repeated requests, and giving the impression that he did not trust Allen, Mario alienated a loyal and potentially valuable employee.

Allen felt so frustrated by not having access to the information he needed to do the kind of management job he was capable of that he decided that the job was no longer worth his full attention and energy. He gave up hope of making a contribution to Mario's company. Instead he decided to give his employer "just what he can appreciate and use [of my talents and skills]."

As a result Mario no longer has a loyal and committed employee. Instead he has turned Allen into the kind of employee described by management expert Tom Peters (1991): "The average person on the front line in your organization is talented, thoughtful, caring, dynamic, and creative, except for the eight hours a day they work for you."

Allen is now using his talent and creativity to develop his own entrepreneurial business, while using his job to "pay the bills." He reports, "I'm not enjoying going to the day job, but I'm grateful to have a regular paycheck." He is working double duty now in order to create challenging and meaningful work for himself in the future.

Mario must figure out how to save his foundering chain of stores without Allen's help. Sadly, he probably has no idea that he has wasted a valuable resource by not being truthful with his managers. He may even fully intend to implement the changes he promised, or believe that he has already done so. It has probably never occurred to him that an employee could be a source of help in his struggle.

Allen feels satisfied with the way he has managed this uncomfortable situation. He believes he did the very best he could to help his employer. Now that his employer has demonstrated an unwillingness to make full use of Allen as an employee, Allen feels perfectly justified in withdrawing his energy from the situation. He now maintains his sense of integrity by holding himself to Mario's standards of job performance while using his real energy to work toward his own business. He does what Mario expects of him but no more. He reasons that Mario will never know what he is missing, and would not appreciate it if it was offered to him again.

When he did not simply follow the orders of upper management but requested a meeting instead, Allen took what he considered to be a necessary risk. He risked his job, rather than risk his integrity. Now he faces another risk: losing his sense of self-worth by staying in a job where he is not valued. He is being truthful to his own values by developing his own business.

Resolving Dilemmas About Maintaining Your Integrity

If you are faced with a dilemma in which you must choose between following instructions and maintaining your integrity, these guidelines will help.

1. Examine the situation as creatively as possible and search for additional alternatives. Sometimes discussing the problem with everyone who is involved and inviting their ideas will generate new options. At other times, an outside opinion might bring a fresh perspective.

When Allen felt very isolated and frustrated, he sought support from acquaintances on the Internet, people he knew were interested in creating healthy organizations. Instead of giving up, he kept seeking new options.

2. When you discover additional possibilities, communicate them to the person who has the authority to make the required decision. Include as much information as you can about the reasons behind your suggestions.

Nonetheless, you may discover that the decision maker has concerns or agendas that you do not know about and cannot address. He or she may or may not be truthful about these issues, and your suggestion may not be acceptable under the circumstances. If you come to the conclusion that you cannot resolve your dilemma, consider the following options.

3. Think about how you can maintain your own integrity given the circumstances. What obligations do you need to fulfill in order to feel at peace with yourself? Is there an honorable way to renegotiate these obligations?

Allen knew that his first contractual obligation was to his employer. He also felt a moral obligation to protect his employees and his customers. He could not carry out the directives of upper management to misrepresent the reasons for closing his store, and still be at peace with himself. Since he was unwilling to follow these orders, he needed to inform Mario about his decision to disobey and then attempt to renegotiate.

4. If you feel you cannot maintain your own integrity in a given situation, think through the likely short- and long-term

consequences of refusing to compromise. Decide if you are willing to refuse an assignment or resign your position, if necessary. Obviously, this will not be an easy decision. The risks may be more than you think you can manage, and you may decide to compromise, after all. Only you can decide.

Allen knew he might lose his job by refusing to tell the story Mario wanted told. There was also the possibility that he would lose his job in several months when the outlet closed, although he suspected that he would be offered another job within the company if he followed the party line. *Allen wanted to keep his job but decided that keeping his integrity by telling his truth was his only acceptable option.* His best option may or may not be your best option.

5.   Think through your decision carefully. It might help to write lists of the potential financial and emotional costs and benefits of every option you can think of. Then share your list with someone you trust. Ask that person to suggest additional possibilities.

6.   Thomas Leonard, founder of Coach University, suggests that you make decisions by considering your integrity first, then your needs, and then your preferences. Telling yourself the truth about each of these areas will help you make the best possible choice in uncomfortable circumstances.

Reference

Peters, T. J. "Tom Peters Live." Audiotape. Boulder, Colo.: Career Track Publications, 1991.

CHAPTER

9

Sometimes It Makes Sense Not to Tell the Truth

Marjorie, age forty-eight, probably would have lost her job if anyone learned that she had not actually graduated from high school. Since she was getting outstanding reviews for her work, she decided to keep her secret to herself and continue to work with the difficult clients at a group home for people with special needs.

Marjorie loved her job caring for developmentally disabled adults in a residential care program. She cooked, cleaned, and cared for the physical and emotional needs of her charges. She was often assigned particularly difficult clients that other staff members had trouble managing, because for some reason these residents responded to her. Despite her success, Marjorie worried about keeping her job.

When she consulted the agency's Employee Assistance Program (EAP) office and was assured of confidentiality, she finally admitted the reason for her worries. Twenty years before, when she had originally applied to work for the agency, she had been desperate to get a job. Knowing that a high school diploma was required for the position she wanted, Marjorie had lied and written down that she had completed two years of college, but she was actually a high-school dropout.

Back then she had worked for the agency for a few years and then moved to another state. Fifteen years later, Marjorie came back and reapplied for a job with the same agency. Fearing discovery, she repeated her lies on her new job application. Now she was troubled. The first time she lied, lying seemed natural and appropriate. Now that she was more mature, and had teenagers of her own, she had come to value telling the truth. At the same time she needed this job and did not want to risk being fired.

When the EAP counselor questioned her about her history, Marjorie admitted that she had been an incorrigible teenager, that she had spent much of that period of her life in correctional and mental institutions. Marjorie volunteered that the reason she loved her job so much was that she could identify with the residents. Her ability to empathize with the residents allowed her to sense needs they could not communicate to other members of the staff. When she responded to their unspoken needs, even the most difficult clients would cooperate with her.

Even with all the evidence of her success on her job, Marjorie was feeling guilty and uncertain about living a lie. Being familiar with the bureaucracy of the organization, the counselor was quite certain that Marjorie would lose her job if she admitted to lying. He also knew that Marjorie was performing a valuable service exceptionally well, and that the agency was having difficulty retaining good employees to do this work. He thought that if Marjorie were to tell the truth now, the outcome would be nothing but damage to everyone concerned—herself, her clients, the agency, and her family.

The counselor helped Marjorie understand that the reason for the requirement was to assure a certain level of competency among employees, and that Marjorie had certainly demonstrated that she was capable of doing her job competently. She also demonstrated competency on an ongoing basis by easily completing the regular training classes that were required to maintain her position. He told her that it was extremely unlikely that anyone would ever ask her any questions about her education, and that he did not believe that anyone would be harmed if she did not tell anyone else about the old lie. Marjorie felt relieved after their discussion and decided to keep her secret, and her job.

Can Truth-Telling Do More Harm Than Good?

In certain instances, telling the truth can be inviting disaster. Yet you may say that that belief, unexamined, is what often stops us from telling the truth in any uncomfortable situation. What we can learn from Marjorie's situation is that it is critical that you think carefully about each situation and the probable consequences of truth-telling, instead of responding automatically. In some instances the compromise of "don't ask, don't tell" avoids creating a situation where all parties would be forced to take action that would cause more harm than good.

A basic ethical principle of the medical profession is to do no harm. This is a useful guideline to follow, as long as you look at who will be harmed by the truth. Many physicians used to believe that it would be harmful to inform a patient that he or she had only a short time to live. In many cases it actually would have been very uncomfortable for everyone *but* the patient to discuss impending death. Now most physicians know that many patients actually prefer to know the truth in order to make appropriate preparations. Still, each decision must be made on an individual basis.

Marjorie's counselor used the same principle to help her think about the impact of telling the truth about her background. Many people probably would have been harmed if Marjorie had tried to correct an earlier lie. In a sense, Marjorie was harming only herself by feeling anxious and guilty about maintaining the deception. With the help of the counselor, she concluded that not telling the truth would limit additional harm to herself and others.

Alcoholics Anonymous and other Twelve Step programs (1953) invoke a similar principle. Although participants are encouraged to make "amends" or restitution to others they have harmed by past behavior, they are cautioned that amends should not be made if doing so would cause further harm to others.

Making amends means different things to different people. Our court system often recommends a penalty of delivering service to the community to make amends for breaking laws or causing damage. Marjorie, doing a difficult low-paying job with love and devotion, certainly contributed more of benefit to the community than any harm she might have caused through her deception. Understanding this truth helped relieve her guilt.

If you need to decide whether it makes sense to withhold the truth in a given situation, think over the matter carefully. Like others who have wrestled with this dilemma, you will need to consider the needs of others, the realities of the situation, as well as your own needs, before reaching any conclusions. Here are some questions you can think about as you assess your options.

1. *Ask yourself, "What are the implications of my choice?"* Jim believed that his opportunities for advancement in the company would be severely limited if anyone knew that he was actually financially independent and did not need his job. He chose not to share that information.

2. *What kind of damage do you believe will occur if you tell the truth?* Ian believed that if his team discovered that he was investigating other employment opportunities, they would feel betrayed, and their work on the project would suffer. He kept his secret and eventually decided not to make a move.

3. *Who will be protected if you keep the truth hidden?* Janet knew that one of her coworkers was trying to divorce an abusive husband. When the husband called her and asked questions about her friend's activities, Janet lied and told him that she did not have the information he demanded.

4. *How are you making your predictions? Are they based on fear of embarrassment or on solid information about the system in which you are functioning?* Yvonne served in the military. As a lesbian, she honored the "don't ask, don't tell" rule and was careful not to call attention to her sexual preference.

There are no formulas and no right answers. What is absolutely right for one person is absolutely wrong for another in a similar situation. If you can, discuss the situation with a trusted friend. If necessary, talk with a professional. Only you can make the choice.

How to Decide Whether or Not to Tell the Truth

Making lists of the benefits and drawbacks of telling the truth can be very helpful in coming to a decision.

1. Write a list of the positive things you believe could happen if you tell the truth in your situation. How you or others may feel afterward also belongs on each list.

2. Write a list of the positive things you believe could happen if you withhold the truth.

3. Now list the possible negative consequences of telling the truth in this situation.

4. Next list the possible negative consequences of withholding the truth in this situation.

5. Review all your lists, and rate the likelihood of each thing happening. Use a scale of 1–10, where 1 means almost certain *not to* happen, and 10 means almost certain *to* happen.

6. Who or what is being protected if you don't tell the truth? This could be you, your family, a coworker, a boss, a project, a piece of property, and so forth.

7. What harm is likely to occur to whomever or whatever you are trying to protect if you do tell the truth?

8. If you do not tell the truth, what will you need to do to assuage your conscience in this situation? Will you need to make amends in some way?

9. If you are still uncertain about what to do, review this exercise with a trusted advisor.

Reference

Anonymous. *Twelve Steps and Twelve Traditions.* New York: Alcoholics Anonymous World Services, 1953.

PART TWO

Tools for Becoming a
Truth Teller

Consultant Rick Huttner is a truth teller. He earns his living and the respect of his clients by telling them the truth about why their businesses are not profitable, and what to do about it. Often these truths are painful, yet Rick has a way of presenting his analysis of their problems that makes the truth acceptable to his clients.

Rick explains, "It does not help to tell people what I know until they are willing to hear it. What I do is work to build rapport and trust. I know that when I work with people, it is imperative that I honor who they are and what they have done. I respect all the input they give me. I listen for what they really want from their lives. I have learned that to do my job I have to be authentically who I am. It [sharing the truth] is really listening, listening, listening and at the appropriate time adding something to the conversation, and then change happens."

Becoming a truth teller involves a series of challenges. First you must exchange seeing the world as you would like it to be for seeing the world as it is. Once you are able to see beyond your illusions, your next challenge becomes learning to communicate what you see to others in a way that they can accept. To do this you need to learn that others may see the world, and the truth, differently than you do.

Your most difficult challenge may be to help others to hear your truth. To do this, you must learn to listen and understand their perceptions before you share your own. As you and others become more skillful, you may then create an entirely new understanding of the "truth" between you.

It becomes easier to tell your truth when you assume that *at any given moment you and others are doing the best you can to get what you think you need, using the resources available to you.* When you accept that almost everyone is struggling to get what he or she needs, you can appreciate that there is often a positive intention behind even the most unskilled and deceptive behavior. When you understand this, you may find it easier to meet the challenges of learning to become a truth teller.

You may not always need what you think you need. When you were a child, you needed to be safe; as an adult you can decide what kind of risks you can accept. Asking the question "What am I trying to get in this situation?" helps you uncover what you think you need. Then you can decide whether continuing to try to meet that need is an appropriate goal in the situation.

If you can use only old familiar resources and tools, then you limit your options to achieve your goals. Adding the skills that others have used to understand what is true for them and to communicate that truth to others can help you develop a rich tool bag of resources to help you become a successful truth teller.

To learn these skills you must decide to risk letting both yourself and others know that you are not perfect. You aren't, and neither are they. Many people are relieved when they accept their own and others' imperfections simply as part of our shared humanity. Everyone whose story is shared in this section has accepted that risk!

Once you have accepted this risk, you can learn the skills that help you to share your perceptions while minimizing the risk of hurting or embarrassing others. By studying these stories you can learn to present information so that others can accept it without becoming upset or defensive.

These stories are about real people who have successfully learned to tell the truth to themselves and others. They all had experienced fear and went ahead anyhow. They might not have loved the results, but they all felt that the risk was worth the reward of increased self-esteem, better understanding of others, successful completion of projects, better communication skills, more productive meetings, and a more supportive and rewarding workplace.

Some of the people and companies who were willing to let the truth about their struggles serve as an example for others are identified by name here. In other instances, revealing names might cause embarrassment or harm to others; those identities are concealed.

When a company or an individual makes a commitment to truth-telling, and devotes resources to developing the skills necessary to help individuals recognize their own truths and to communicate them with awareness and compassion, the results can be startling. Teamwork, synergy, innovation, and responsiveness increase. Trust, loyalty, and self-esteem develop. Turnover decreases, and profits expand. WHY NOT take the risk of learning to tell the truth?

CHAPTER
10

Examining Assumptions

Kathleen believed her boss was behaving inappropriately at meetings they attended together. She felt that she could not confront him without jeopardizing her position. When she carefully examined her own discomfort, it dawned on her that her assumptions and objectives might be very different from his.

Kathleen was appalled by the behavior of her boss, Jeff, the president and chief operating officer of the high-tech company where she worked. Nine months after accepting a position as vice president of the firm, she found herself seriously considering resigning. On one occasion she was particularly frustrated, because she actually heard Jeff divulging "secret" company information to potential partners who were also current competitors. Furthermore, she thought that he was misrepresenting the truth by implying that certain informal verbal agreements were actually signed contracts.

Kathleen knew that she was becoming so judgmental about Jeff's behavior that she might not be thinking clearly enough to handle the situation appropriately. Whenever she thought of confronting him directly, she had difficulty deciding just what her objectives would be. She just knew that she would have represented the company very differently in the negotiations if she had been Jeff.

She did not really want to resign. She was committed to the people on her team and excited about the product she was in charge of bringing to market. Furthermore, her salary was excellent, and she was just settling in to the West Coast community where she had relocated for the new job. She was not ready to make another move. She decided that she would be in a better position to explore her options if she consulted someone who had no connection with the company, and she engaged me as her coach.

Kathleen explained that in her move from public administration to the private sector, she had deliberately accepted the challenge of developing her career in a very different environment. We both agreed that she needed to examine the situation more carefully before making any changes. She needed to understand more about the values and expectations of people who held the power in this new culture before she could hope to be effective in influencing them.

When she compared Jeff's behavior with her own in her previous position as the director of an innovative municipal program, Kathleen was puzzled. "I was very enthusiastic and very realistic about both the results and the difficulties of the program when I reported to the public," she told me. "He keeps crossing the line and talking about possibilities as if they were actually happening, and he exaggerates the impact of things that I know are of minor importance. He does not even seem concerned with taking our product to market. I thought that I joined the company to produce results, and he does not seem to care about that at all."

Kathleen tried to see patterns in Jeff's odd behavior. He seemed to be trying to make the company sound better to others than it actually was. He certainly was not focused on selling product. In fact, he did not seem to be focused inside the company at all. He had even told her to lighten up when she communicated her urgency about marketing the product. Then she recalled a statement that seemed especially strange to her. Jeff had told her to "stick with [him], and they would both get rich."

She was certainly in favor of getting rich, but she did not think Jeff's current direction would accomplish that goal. Everything Jeff was doing seemed to run opposite to what she considered the path to success. Her philosophy was to develop great products, take them to market, and create revenue for the company. She valued representing the company as accurately and honestly as possible to potential joint venture partners. His agenda seemed to be to talk about what he hoped would happen as if it had already happened. He seemed to be trying to convince others to join the company because of its potential instead of its actual achievements.

Kathleen's initial impulse was to label Jeff's behavior as unethical. When she thought of him as unethical, it seemed appropriate to resign from her position. When she thought of him as having a different objective than she did, she was not so sure that resigning was necessary.

To explore this further, I encouraged Kathleen to imagine stepping into Jeff's shoes and to think about the situation from his perspective. Sorting through the information she had accumulated about Jeff, Kathleen started musing: "He has a large company mentality. He knows who to play golf with and what to say to get noticed by the community. He has never brought a product to market, but he has increased the street value of companies he has worked with in the past. He focuses on how people perceive us instead of on what we are actually doing. He is extremely concerned about how we are connected with other companies."

Finally the information clicked into another pattern, and Kathleen concluded: "High-tech companies have gone public based on how people perceived them. His main goal must be to take the company public by increasing its value on the street (to investors). He is doing things that he believes will add that kind of value to the company."

Kathleen decided to stay with the company without confronting Jeff about his exaggerations. She accepted the fact that she and Jeff had "different values and beliefs about how things need to work." At the same time, she has not given up her own values and beliefs. Six months later, she reports that she has confronted Jeff about many matters that she believes are essential for adding real value to the company.

Kathleen chooses her battles carefully now, focusing on specific matters she feels need to be addressed so that she can maintain her integrity. She believes that her job as an executive is to "get stuff done," and she is working diligently to move the product forward in the marketplace. She knows that Jeff considers her a "pain in the ass"; he has told her so. Yet he has repeatedly yielded to her point of view, and his respect for her seems to have increased. She enjoys the additional responsibilities he has delegated to her.

She repeatedly reminds herself: "You're not the president of the company. He is!" Then she focuses on the question "What part of the company CAN I run?" She runs her own area according to her own vision. A significant core group in the company affirms her viewpoint and is grateful for her leadership. She says, "Sometimes it would be easier to say I'm not going to get involved, but the only way I can be comfortable with myself is to keep figuring out how to influence the company to do what I believe is in everyone's best interest."

Kathleen is not sure what she will do next. She reports, "I'm still frustrated, and I still may leave. I would be more comfortable in a different culture. I know things would function very differently if I were running the show. Another company is considering buying us, and I know they like my approach. I'm waiting to see what happens."

Unexamined Assumptions Cause Problems

Everyone makes assumptions. Each time you examine a situation, you do so through the filter of your past experiences. When a current situation contains elements that are similar to a situation you have encountered before, your brain quickly decides that similar means "the same as" the last time. As soon as you reach this conclusion and you put this event into a category of events you have responded to successfully in a certain way in the past, you relax. You feel secure because you think you know what to do; you stop thinking about it. After all, why waste energy on a problem that has already been solved?

Often this approach works very well. Somebody who is an expert at anything, from playing bridge to repairing an automobile to running a company, has accumulated a large repertoire of recognized patterns for addressing certain common problems they have encountered many times in the past. By matching a new problem against their extensive background list, they come up with solutions quickly and easily. When the experts' solution does not work, they reexamine the situation and try to find a new and different way of handling it, thereby adding a new pattern to their repertoire.

Unfortunately, it is easy to get stuck trying to make a solution for an old problem fit a new situation. If you believe in your first assessment that this situation is just like an earlier one, and your old solution does not work, you may dig in your heels and try harder to make the old solution work instead of going back and figuring out whether the new situation really is like the old one. It is easier to blame the lack of resolution on someone not "doing it right" than it is to go back and question your original assumption.

A common assumption that causes an unbelievable number and variety of problems is that "everyone in the world is just like me." A corollary to that assumption is that "if they are not just like me, they are wrong." It's easy to understand why this is so common. You grow up inside your own skin and generally have no opportunity to find out how another person experiences the world. Furthermore, you are self-centered for a large part of your childhood. Everyone is. You only learn that others are different when they tell you about the differences, and even then you can only try to understand their point of view.

Many tools that help you determine your personality style, or your listening, management, or learning strategies, are useful because they show you that different people have different ways of approaching the world. They help you understand ordinary differences between people and lead you to reexamine the assumption that everyone else is just like you. When you reexamine your assumptions, you start to think about a given situation in a new way and allow yourself to accept new information that gives you new options for being creative and resolving a problem.

When Kathleen was considering resigning, she was basing her decision on her own unexamined assumptions about the meaning of Jeff's behavior. She started out assuming that his vision for the company was the same as hers. Since his behavior was inconsistent with her vision, she assumed that he must be either unethical or irresponsible. She did not want to work with someone she did not respect (because of his presumed unethical behavior), so resigning seemed to be the appropriate course of action.

When Kathleen examined her assumptions, she recognized that her explanation was only one possible way of interpreting the situation. When she was able to shift her perspective, she could see other explanations that helped her understand Jeff's behavior in a different light. When she assumed that Jeff's primary objective was to increase the market value of the company so that he could take it public, she could see that the behaviors she was questioning were consistent with his seeking that objective. She then made a new assumption: that Jeff was behaving in a way that he believed would be beneficial to the company.

Kathleen did not agree with what she now assumed was Jeff's objective, but when she simply understood his objective to be different from her own, she no longer considered him unethical. She could now accept him as a colleague with a different point of view. With this new perspective, she felt that she could work to achieve her own objectives within the company without undermining his. She came to believe that both she and Jeff wanted to increase the value of the company, but that they did not agree about the best way to achieve their mutual goal.

Today Kathleen still would like for Jeff to adopt her view that it is best for the company to build a firm foundation by delivering excellent products to many customers. Jeff is still trying to achieve one really big success. Kathleen continues to strategically argue for her own vision. She continually assesses "how much more of my truth he can accept today," and she continues to deliver it. For the moment, that is enough.

Examining Your Own Assumptions

Since you tend to stop thinking about something once you reach a conclusion about it, you probably do not realize how much additional information may be available to you. Slowing down the process of reaching conclusions will allow you to increase your access to important truths in any situation.

You can learn to understand how others may experience the world—even without walking a mile in their moccasins. Here are some tools:

1.   Start by assuming that all people, including yourself, are doing the best they can to get what they need in the world at any given moment. While this assumption may not be 100 percent accurate, it is the first step in gaining a useful perspective on the often incomprehensible reasons behind someone else's actions.

2.   Pay close attention to the physical appearance of the person you are trying to understand. Notice details. How tall? How fat or thin? Hairstyle? Makeup? Style and fit of clothing? Condition of clothing—fresh or soiled? Posture? Jewelry? Personal grooming? You probably already notice these details, but you probably do so very quickly, usually reaching instant conclusions without even really registering everything you see.

3.   Try to imagine what it is like to be a person of the gender, shape, and size you have observed. This exercise can be especially interesting if the person's physical characteristics are very different from your own. If you are a large man, imagining yourself in the body of a small woman is a strange experience. Think about needing a ladder to reach a high shelf or frequently needing to tilt your head upward to carry on a conversation. Imagine how the world would appear to you if you were the person you are trying to understand.

4.   Be curious about everything you observe. Instead of judging, ask yourself why someone might make the clothing or grooming choices you have noticed. Try this exercise with a person whose choices you admire; and then try it again with a person whose choices bewilder you (perhaps a trendy teenager with green hair). Of course, you can only guess someone else's

reasons, but even guessing will help you challenge your original assumptions.

5.   To get a sense of what the person you are curious about is feeling, try to imitate his or her posture, movements, and facial expression. If you do this in the other person's presence, do it discreetly. When people are mirrored in this way, they often feel comfortable and at ease. Surprisingly, when you mirror someone physically, your emotions often shift to match theirs as well.

You may already do this unconsciously; many people do. When you are talking with someone you feel comfortable with, take a moment to observe your own physical positions. Often you will find that you have unconsciously matched the other person in the position of your arms, legs, head tilt and so forth. If you would like more information about this fascinating phenomena, read one of a variety of books on Neurolinguistic Programming, which teaches this technique as a way to establish rapport with others. I like *Influencing with Integrity* by Genie Z. Laborde (1984).

6.   Find out as much as you can about the person you are trying to understand. What do you know about his or her family or living situation? What about previous jobs or training? Hometown? How about hobbies and volunteer positions? What about pets? Automobiles? Sports? Anything you can learn that helps you understand how this person is a unique human being will be helpful.

7.   Listen to the words the individual chooses to utter. Often people use the same words to signify very different things. If you are uncertain about what someone means when he or she chooses certain words, ask. For example, when someone says, "You have lots of time," it can mean that you have until this afternoon to complete a task, or it can mean that the deadline is a month away. Be sure to get the specific information you need. It is just fine to ask, "Please tell me when you will need this," or "How long is lots of time?"

8.   Notice what tone of voice the person is using. Does it change under different circumstances? What do you suppose that might mean? What do voice pitch and tempo suggest about the person you are observing?

By engaging in these activities, you will interfere with the automatic process of making quick assumptions about any person or situation. Going through this list will reawaken your natural curiosity and encourage you to gather as much data as possible. The more information you have, the more likely it is that you will discover hidden truth that will help you make appropriate decisions for yourself.

Reference

LaBorde, G. Z. *Influencing with Integrity: Management Skills for Communication and Negotiation.* Palo Alto, Calif.: Syntony Publishing, 1984.

CHAPTER

11

Know Yourself First

Irwin, a telecommunications executive, believed that he just could not find good help. One administrative assistant after another resigned after a few days on the job. It never occurred to him that his demanding behavior was contributing to the problem. He was not aware of how radically his behavior changed after he'd had a few drinks with his lunch. The first time a business associate suggested that he might have a problem with alcohol, he did not listen. It took a near disaster to get his attention. Recalling the situation several years later, Irwin identified it as a major turning point in his life and his career.

When he received a citation for driving under the influence of alcohol, Irwin was irritated. Fortunately, no one had been hurt when his car sideswiped another car as he was returning to his office after lunching with an important client. Irwin told himself that the accident happened when his attention lapsed, because he was fuming about a situation at the office. He knew that once he got back to the office he would have trouble getting his assistant to do the follow-up work from that day's appointment. He was absolutely certain he was not impaired. The blood alcohol test proved otherwise.

When the judge ordered him to attend a class for drunk drivers or forfeit his driver's license, Irwin was embarrassed and angry. After all, he told himself, "I'm no drunk. I have been driving for almost forty years. I know what I'm doing."

Irwin reluctantly participated in the required class, fully prepared to put in his time and then get on with his life. But then a film about accidents caused by drunk drivers captured his attention. One young victim reminded him of his grandson, and as he watched he remembered how his daughter-in-law had refused to allow his own grandchild to ride in his car. His son always managed to drive whenever they went anywhere together. He remembered other recent experiences that had puzzled and irritated him.

He knew that his wife was worried about his health and wanted him to take better care of himself. She kept telling him he was drinking too much, and she urged him to cut back. He also knew that a lot of people at the office were avoiding him. The personnel department was frustrated because they could not provide an administrative assistant who would stay with him. He was "too difficult to work with." Reluctantly he remembered his associate, Max, suggesting that his use of alcohol was causing problems at the office. At the time that Max made the comment, Irwin had angrily denied any problems. Now he was not so sure.

Once he accepted the idea that he might have a problem with alcohol, Irwin decided to stop drinking for at least three months. This was not particularly difficult. He had enjoyed drinking socially for many years, and he had only recently started having several cocktails at lunch. Stopping drinking was the easy part. Accepting the truth about how close he had come to irrevocably damaging his life and his career was more challenging.

Once he stopped drinking, Irwin noticed that his office was littered with incomplete projects. As he reviewed them, he realized that they were not up to his usual high standards. In fact, he felt embarrassed when he began to think that some of his colleagues had already seen his deterioration. Since Max had spoken to him about the problem, Irwin decided to confide in him. Telling Max about his driving citation and the class, Irwin thanked him for his concern and apologized for not listening sooner. He then asked Max for the feedback he had ignored earlier.

Max, whose father was a recovering alcoholic, told Irwin that he had noticed changes in Irwin's behavior during the past year. "You used to be very easy to get along with," Max confided, "but for the past six months the only time we could count on a civil response from you was in the morning. Most afternoons your personality would change. You would become a bear, growling and shouting at anyone who crossed you in the slightest way. Your administrative assistants took the worst of it. No wonder they asked for transfers. I saw at least two of them in tears after they left your office."

Irwin was shocked. He knew he had been irritable, but he had no idea that his behavior had been so out of control. No wonder people had been avoiding him. He decided that he needed feedback from his family, too, and cautiously asked them if he had caused them any problems. They were reluctant to share much, but his wife invited him to join her in a session with her counselor. There he learned that his family was afraid that he was an alcoholic and did not trust that he would keep his commitment to stop drinking.

The counselor suggested that Irwin continue to see her, and he agreed. Her professional feedback helped him learn to recognize his emotional blind spots. He learned that his fears about losing his position were neither unmasculine nor unrealistic. He also learned that talking realistically about his fears helped him to make contingency plans to protect himself and his family. Several months later Irwin decided that alcohol really was not the problem. Hiding his emotional vulnerability even from himself had caused him to use alcohol inappropriately. He chose to start drinking socially again, and now he never has more than two drinks in an evening. He avoids alcohol at lunch, and over the past five years he has not had any additional problems. What Irwin does not avoid any longer is feedback. He welcomes it and even seeks it out. If someone suggests that a problem exists, he asks for elaboration, takes it very seriously, and does whatever is necessary to learn the truth about himself.

What You Don't Know Can Hurt You

In 1963 two creative thinkers originated a tool that has been widely used to help promote more truthfulness in the workplace, the Jo-Hari Window (Luft 1963). It helps clarify the relationships between information we have about ourselves and information others have about us. The theory suggests that the more we understand and appreciate ourselves and each other, the better our working relationships will be (Figure 11.1).

Some areas of our lives are known to ourselves and others. These public truths may appear on our résumés or in the company newsletter. For instance, anyone could have called Irwin's company and learned his job title. There is some information about ourselves that we consider private. We hide this information from others by choice. It may be private medical information, or the opinions we have about others, or the balance in our savings account. We can usually choose if, how, when, and to whom we reveal this information. Choosing to reveal this information is a form of truth-telling that is under our own control.

A great deal of information that we would like to keep private is a matter of public record, or it is stored and exchanged through

		FEEDBACK	
		Known to Self	Unknown to Self
D I S C L O S U R E	Known to Others	Public Area	Blind Area
	Unknown to Others	Hidden Area	Unknown Area

Figure 11.1 **The Jo-Hari Window: what we and others do and don't know about ourselves.**

computer networks. If you have any doubt about the truth of this, just subscribe to a magazine that is outside of your usual interests, and watch how quickly your junk mail reflects your new choice.

Usually the availability of this information is not a problem, because no one else chooses to search out our hidden information. But as people in the public eye have learned to their dismay, much private information is available and can be made public against their wishes. Irwin wanted to keep his drunk-driving citation a secret from his company and his family. Since it was not reported in the press, he managed to keep his secret until he was ready to share it.

There is also information about us that neither we nor anyone else knows about. This unknown information includes our potential ability to master things we haven't yet attempted. It also includes undiscovered interests and talents that are revealed only under certain circumstances. Until Irwin began to talk with the counselor, Irwin's fears were not known to either himself or anyone else.

Everybody has blind spots. You have certain tendencies that you yourself are not aware of but that others can see. These are your blind spots, and they can cause big problems. For instance, Irwin could not see how alcohol was affecting his behavior. Over two hundred years ago, Scottish poet Robert Burns (Kinsley 1968) wrote:

> *Oh wad some power the giftie gie us*
> *To see oursel's as others see us!*
> *It wad frae monie a blunder free us,*
> *And foolish notion.*

It can be a real challenge to try to see ourselves as others see us. Sometimes we actually can do so, by watching ourselves on videotape, or listening to an audiotape. Usually, though, this information is only available when others are willing to share it with us. Many of us have a blind spot about being alerted to our blind spot, so we turn away any feedback that does not agree with our own self-assessments.

Sometimes the information relates to a language pattern or a habit that annoys others. We would happily change it if only we knew it existed. Sometimes the information is extremely important to us, because a certain weakness may keep us from career advancement or interfere with important relationships. We may not exactly welcome feedback that brings disconcerting information to our attention, but we can learn to accept these new truths about ourselves. Once we become aware of this new information, it moves from the blind area to the public area, and we can then make desirable changes.

This feedback can also reveal skills and talents we are unaware of. Each time someone compliments us specifically about something we have done well, we may learn a little more about ourselves. When we learn to accept any feedback as a gift, we can use it to fuel our growth and development.

Sometimes this feedback is so contrary to our beliefs about ourselves that we refuse to believe or accept it. Irwin did not want to believe that he had a problem with alcohol. Disbelief at this level of intensity is called denial. It is a self-protective mechanism that persists until some very strong confrontation forces us to accept an unpleasant truth. Once we accept the difficult feedback, we must choose whether or not to change.

How to Use Feedback to Reduce Your Blind Spot

1.   Accept the fact that you are not perfect and that nobody else is perfect, either. This seems self-evident, but a surprising number of people expect themselves to get everything right the first time, often without instruction. If you are extremely self-critical, you may be one of these uncomfortable individuals. Feedback often offers information about your imperfections.

2.   Drop your defensiveness. Feedback feels like criticism to many people. When you are tempted to respond to feedback by explaining why you behaved as you did, and why you could not possibly have done anything differently, stop yourself. Take a deep breath and listen carefully. Think about what is being said to you; try not to think about how you need to respond. Being able to do this will take courage and practice.

3.   Make sure you understand what you are being told. Ask questions about specifics. Ask for details and examples, and listen to them.

4.   Restate in your own words your understanding of the issues that are being discussed, and clarify the issues before you respond to them. Clarify whether the person offering the feedback is requesting that you take some action in response to the feedback. Showing that you are listening and understanding is often enough.

5.   Decide whether a response is really necessary. If it is, take time to think about how to respond, even if it means asking to discuss the situation at a later time.

6.   Recognize that even criticism usually contains useful information. What you are hearing may be about you, or it may be about the needs and feelings of the person criticizing you. Even criticism that does not have your best interests at heart can help you relate better to the person who is "attacking" you. Treat criticism as feedback offered in an unskilled manner, and respond to it as if it is offered as a gift. This takes practice—do the best you can.

7.   Always thank the person offering you feedback.

8.   If you suspect that someone has information about you or your behavior and is not offering to share it with you, ask for that person's feedback. Be certain to accept the comments nondefensively and with appreciation, even if you are unhappy with what is being said. The more often you do this, the more you will learn about yourself.

9.   Once more, say thank you and mean it!

References

Kinsley, J. *The Poems and Songs of Robert Burns*. Oxford: Clarendon, 1968.

Luft, J. *Group Process: An Introduction to Group Dynamics*. Palo Alto, Calif.: National Press, 1963.

CHAPTER

12

Do You Recognize the Signals
You Send Yourself?

*After five years of helping my business partner/husband pro-
duce and market an intensive four-day workshop retreat while
maintaining a professional practice and managing our company, I burned out. I felt so depressed that one morning I did
not want to get out of bed. That symptom finally got my attention, and I realized that I hated parts of what I was doing.
Telling the truth meant risking the destruction of our thirteen-
year-old business.*

This is a very personal story. In retrospect, it is hard to believe
how many mistakes I made and how many signals I ignored before
I was able to know my own truth. I learned a lot from this experience, and I have no regrets.

In 1980 my husband, Jon, and I accidentally changed the nature
and direction of our business. We did not think about or discuss

the implications of a business decision we made together; we simply responded to an opportunity to make a stimulating and effective training opportunity available to our clients and associates. We had spent the previous eight years teaching and practicing Transactional Analysis psychotherapy locally and nationally, as well as consulting with business and educational professionals about applying Transactional Analysis in the workplace.

Always alert for new ideas and technology to help ourselves and our clients, we eagerly participated in a variety of learning experiences. We felt so excited and enlivened after participating in one seminar that we invited the leader, Jason, to present it to our community. Because of our enthusiasm it was easy to enroll fifty people for the five-day residential workshop. We managed the logistics, handled the finances, and answered questions while teaching and maintaining our regular practice. Our small office was almost overwhelmed, but we enjoyed the excitement.

The response to the workshop was so enthusiastic that when Jason's business partner suggested producing a second workshop, Jon, our office manager, and several other workshop participants wanted to proceed. I had misgivings and a vague feeling of unease that I could not clearly articulate. Each time I raised an objection, I was told that I just did not fully understand the fabulous potential of the program. I decided to put my fears aside, and we made the fateful decision to produce a second workshop.

We were hooked into what, in retrospect, was clearly an addictive experience. Over the next five years we produced twenty-five major workshops. Enrolling and managing the workshops consumed an increasing amount of our time and resources. We installed expensive new office systems to manage the workflow. My husband devoted much of his time to managing the production activities while I struggled to keep up with our other business activities.

The finances were not really working, and I knew it. The cash flow certainly increased, but our bottom line remained basically unchanged. All the extra cash went to support production activities. On paper the workshops looked as if they were profitable, as long as the office overhead was not considered a workshop expense. If we had included the overhead we would have realized that our (my) other activities were subsidizing the workshops. I had a strong intuitive sense that something was wrong, but I bowed to the argument that our office overhead would continue whether or not we were producing the workshops.

Because of my uneasiness, I attempted to control the seminar expenses and activities. I was repeatedly accused of "coming from scarcity." I began to accept other people's beliefs about me, and as a result I felt less and less sure about my own perceptions. Others promised that the financial payoff would come eventually. I kept trying to accept their reassurances, but the numbers still did not make sense to me.

Meanwhile, the participants were thrilled with their experiences. Everyone but me seemed to be having a wonderful time, so I decided that I must have a problem. I tried even harder to be enthusiastic, but I was growing more and more tired. My over-responsible behavior was bringing enough psychotherapy and consulting business into the office to keep us financially viable. We were never in financial danger. We had enough, but all of us were working harder and harder to produce the same financial results.

By this time, Jason had developed additional workshops. One focused on intense personal growth experiences. I was uncomfortable with this from a professional standpoint, because Jon and I had far more expertise with facilitating personal growth than Jason did. I noticed that the workshop participants were enthusiastically flying a thousand miles to consult with Jason about personal problems. Jason never suggested that they consult us for help, even when we requested that he do so.

Increasingly upset and confused, I pulled back from workshop activities and focused on marketing our own psychotherapy services. I would go along to the resorts where the programs were held, but I'd stay in my room and write or design teaching materials while others were enjoying upbeat music and intense emotional experiences. I hated being the spoilsport, but I could not muster much excitement of my own, so I decided to stay out of the way.

Jon remained enthusiastic about the program and decided to join the advanced training programs. I enjoyed some of the national meetings, and many of the people I met became good friends. I had some exciting experiences, but on my own I would not have chosen to spend my time that way. I was still tired.

One morning in 1984 I was shocked to discover that I did not want to get out of bed. That finally got my attention. I recognized the clinical symptoms of depression and burnout. I finally realized that I hated many of the things I was doing each day. I still enjoyed teaching and doing psychotherapy, but I felt that everything else was suffocating me.

I felt terrified. Jon loved the workshops, and was committed to them. We had been married for twenty-four years and in business together for thirteen years. I could not imagine how I could take care of myself without destroying the business, the marriage, or both. I knew the program was valuable for him and for many other people. It just was not right for me. My style was different; and instead of honoring that difference and following my own direction, as I always encouraged others to do, I had been trying to fit myself into someone else's mold. It would not work. I did not fit.

After considerable thought, I decided I had to tell Jon *my* truth. I told him about my problem, and I said that I had reached the conclusion that I needed to withdraw from all activities that supported the workshop business. I told him that he was welcome to continue to do the workshop, but that I needed to concentrate on doing psychotherapy and teaching.

Jon did not like my decision, but he accepted it. About two months later he decided that without my support he no longer wanted to produce the workshop. Two different groups of workshop graduates wanted to purchase that part of our business. We wanted to sell it to the group we thought was most capable of managing it, but Jason preferred the other group. Finally Jason offered to purchase the business himself, so that he could sell it to the group he wanted to work with.

Several workshop graduates who were astute businesspeople helped us negotiate a contract for the sale and transfer of the business. We agreed to turn over the business to Jason's group before the contract was signed, so that they could maintain the continuity of the activities that had already enrolled people. The contract was drawn, as agreed. We signed it and returned it to Jason for his signature.

We did not hear from Jason again for five years. The new "owners" gave us a small payment of approximately 1 percent of the price that Jason had agreed to pay us. After a short time their business collapsed.

Jason's partner later acquired rights to the workshop, brought in new leaders, and created a very successful business. We still believe that the program is extremely valuable and refer people to it when we can. It is no longer produced in our city.

Within the next six months, our own practice did very well. With both of us focused on our own business, and without the workshop production expenses, our profits increased dramatically. My original enthusiasm and energy returned, and our reflection on our five-year adventure led us to exciting new personal and professional discoveries.

Codependency and Other Addictions

When we tried to understand what had caused us to make such unwise business decisions, we found answers by learning to understand addictive behaviors. Addictions are powerful pulls toward certain experiences, tempting people to ignore other important aspects of their lives. Any addiction starts with an attraction. Some substance or experience produces a pleasurable effect. At first both of us were attracted by the intense emotions of joy and excitement we experienced while learning useful information the first time we attended the workshop. We wanted to re-create the experience for ourselves by sharing it with our community. We accomplished that goal by producing the first workshop.

An addiction occurs when someone needs more and more of something (it can be a drug or almost any activity) to produce the same highly desirable result. This is especially true if the desired result is an alteration in mood. Eventually the activity of seeking more and more of the thing, whether it is alcohol or excitement, becomes a problem in itself. Other valued behavior is squeezed out by the intense focus on the activities needed to produce the mood alteration.

When we were invited to keep producing the workshop, the promised reward became financial. The hidden promise was that we would be able to re-create the excitement through the enrollment process and the participation in future workshops. Once we thought we could have all that fun and money, too, the addictive process had begun.

The substance we were attracted to was the adrenaline rush of excitement produced by participating in an emotional experience led by a charismatic teacher. Producing the workshop became the activity we used to seek the excitement. This activity became a problem when it overshadowed all of our other valued activities. Jason's addiction to the pleasure of being admired by his followers led him to promise more and more until he became unable to deliver what he promised.

Jon developed an addiction to the excitement and good feelings generated by the workshops. After a short time, I was no longer interested in this kind of excitement. Yet even though I was a card-carrying feminist, my emotional expectations of myself were that I needed to keep my husband happy. I became addicted to protecting our relationship by helping him to get that experience we both thought he needed. For a long time, it did not occur to me that helping him was detrimental to my own well-being.

Because of our long-term relationship and my family and cultural history, I was susceptible to deciding that my own needs were less important than his. As a young woman growing up in a Jewish family, my mother repeatedly told me about the sacrifices I would need to make to do a good job of keeping my future husband happy. She implied that doing this would make me happy too, so I felt that something was wrong with me when I could not seem to feel satisfied by making sure that he was satisfied. Then I compounded the problem by making a common mistake: I tried harder to satisfy him (a sign of my own addiction to the relationship). As I became overresponsible about making sure that I was supporting what he wanted, I became less and less certain about my own sense of reality. Together we created a codependent relationship.

In a codependent relationship, both partners agree that the needs and feelings of one of the partners are more important than the needs of the other (Weiss and Weiss 1989). In our case, we were both in agreement that Jon's needs for stimulation and excitement were more important than my needs for security and balance. When I began to attend to my own internal signals of discomfort,

I finally acknowledged that something was very wrong. I realized that I had ignored the signals for a long time, both because they were subtle, and because I was caught in supporting Jon's workshop addiction with my codependent behavior.

Either partner can put an end to codependent aspects of a relationship by taking an action that indicates that both parties' needs are equally important. In our case, I decided that I had to focus on my own interests, I decided that my needs were as important as Jon's. When I withdrew my support for his habit, he decided it was too much trouble to continue without my help, and we were both able to reestablish our own individuality and function well together again.

Our growing understanding of the problems that are associated with addiction led us in a direction that enhanced our therapy practice. We wrote a book together, *Recovery from Co-Dependency: It's Never Too Late to Reclaim Your Childhood* (Weiss and Weiss 1989), in which we applied our expertise to the needs of a large new group of clients. Our practice thrived, and we taught the material to many people. The disaster I feared became a launching platform for new growth and success.

How to Escape When You're Trapped in Codependency

1. Pay attention to your own feelings of discomfort. Even if you do not understand why, you may have a hunch or "gut feeling" that something is wrong. Honor that feeling instead of pretending it does not exist.

2. Do something to try to understand the reason for the feeling. Think about it or write about it. Consult with someone you trust about the possible reasons for your feeling. Don't give up.

3. If you cannot find someone to confirm your hunch, make some notes about your situation then put them aside to review at a later time.

4. If you begin to doubt your own perceptions and your own self-worth, suspect that you are caught in a situation where

you are not taking care of yourself. Think about what you need to feel comfortable. Take action to get what you need.

5. If you notice that it is taking more and more of any one thing just to stay even, suspect an addictive situation. If you are too close to the situation to view it objectively, ask for help from a professional who understands addictive behaviors.

6. Remember, it is almost never too late to tell your own truth about any situation. The risk of not taking action may be just as great as the disaster you fear will occur if you tell the truth. Growth is rarely possible without risk.

Reference
Weiss, L., and J. Weiss. *Recovery from Co-Dependency: It's Never Too Late to Reclaim Your Childhood.* Deerfield Beach, Fla.: Health Communications, 1989.

CHAPTER

13

Use Your Intuition to Guide You

Elizabeth embarrassed herself by occasionally crying at faculty committee meetings. She rarely understood the reason for her tears. Usually she would cry when she was asked to comment on something on which everyone else seemed to agree. When the team hired a consultant, he suggested that the entire group examine the situation more carefully. They discovered that Elizabeth's intuition was warning her when something subtle was wrong with some proposed action.

Elizabeth, a civil engineer, had joined the nine-person cross-discipline faculty of the newly created environmental studies program in a medium-sized university. She and the other faculty members were on a committee charged with creating the curriculum for the new degree program, and they were in trouble. Elizabeth very much wanted to contribute to the team, but she often found herself struggling to express her perceptions of the problems the faculty needed to solve. One of the most serious problems was the functioning of the team itself. There had been so much difficulty in forging a working team with professionals from different disciplines that the committee was almost three months behind schedule, and part of the program needed to be operational by the following semester.

A consultant was hired to help develop an effective work team. After the group had a series of meetings with the consultant, a new level of trust began to emerge. As team members expressed their deep commitments to their work and began to function synergistically, Elizabeth sometimes felt emotional. Tears would come to her eyes, and she would blink them away as she attempted to look cool and professional.

During one meeting that seemed to be moving very slowly, Elizabeth began to cry. Embarrassed, she attempted to excuse herself in order to regain her composure, but the consultant encouraged her to stay and to try to articulate the reason for her tears. All she could manage to say was "Something feels wrong."

The consultant asked other team members if they were aware of some problem. At first everyone was quiet. Finally, another team member revealed that he was having difficulty concentrating because he had just learned that his wife might be seriously ill. All of the team members then expressed their concern and support. They talked for a few minutes about how important their families were to them, and how fragile all life was. After this uncharacteristically intimate conversation, someone suggested a coffee break. When the meeting resumed, the work was accomplished astonishingly quickly.

The consultant was very aware of Elizabeth's occasional emotional responses and believed that she was perceiving subtle information that others were not picking up. He suggested that those emotional responses might be signs that Elizabeth had some sort of heightened awareness. Since little is understood about this type of awareness, it is generally labeled intuition. He suggested to the team that Elizabeth's intuitive information might be valuable to them at other times. The team decided that they would like to experiment with that possibility.

Elizabeth agreed to stop trying to ignore her emotions, and the entire group agreed to redirect their attention to how the team was functioning whenever Elizabeth started to cry. Elizabeth was still embarrassed by the situation. She had spent most of her life trying to control her emotions in order to be taken seriously. Now that she was functioning in a professional capacity, it seemed strange to consider her emotions important enough to warrant interrupting work activities.

The first time the team used Elizabeth's tears as a signal of a problem was when the faculty members were discussing purchasing a very expensive software package from a particular vendor, and there seemed to be general agreement about making the purchase. Elizabeth could not imagine why the situation was problematic, but the team members decided to examine the purchasing arrangements more closely. Three team members admitted that they were slightly uneasy about the vendor they had chosen, but because others were satisfied, they had not voiced their doubts. When they checked the vendor's references more closely, they discovered both delivery and servicing problems with the package they had chosen. What the team came to call Elizabeth's early warning system served them well. They chose a different vendor.

Another time, after Elizabeth and her teammates had developed more confidence in her warning system, she arrived at a meeting late and almost immediately felt like crying. She alerted the team, and they switched their focus from the program design they were discussing to the process they were using to make their decision. This time Elizabeth's emotional barometer uncovered a deep resentment one team member had developed about a decision made by another. Once the interpersonal problem was exposed, it was easy to resolve.

The other faculty members came to rely on Elizabeth's intuition as much as they relied on her technical expertise and ability to creatively visualize how to achieve their goals. Elizabeth was delighted to acknowledge that her seemingly out-of-control emotions were actually signaling perceptive abilities that could be of help to the committee. The curriculum was ready on time, and the faculty, willing to examine and tell the truth about its own process, became a model for others to emulate.

Putting Faith in Intuition

Intuitions, gut feelings, hunches, suspicions, premonitions, inklings, educated guesses, insights, visions—all are important resources we all possess. When facts and logical analysis are unavailable or insufficient, we can use our own inner resources to guide us. This ability to perceive information nonlogically and nonlinearly is sometimes known as having a sixth sense, playing it by ear, or having business acumen.

From time to time almost everyone experiences possessing information without having any clear understanding of where it comes from. It usually comes from what may be called our intuitive mind. This is the part of our brains that rapidly processes multiple layers of complex information and instantly recognizes patterns. Our brains automatically compare those patterns with our past experiences and, based upon this information, we jump to conclusions about ourselves, others, situations, and the world.

The whole process happens so quickly and automatically that we are not even aware of it. All we know is that we are attracted or repulsed by a particular opportunity or event. Often we are not even consciously aware of the decisions we reach. Our body may signal these conclusions by tightening muscles, causing a backache or a bellyache. We may feel butterflies (a gut feeling), or a pain in the neck, or a headache. We may feel our hearts pounding or a light-headed sense of relief or joy. We may feel like crying like Elizabeth did. Any of these sensations may be a signal that our intuitive mind is at work and that it has a message for us.

You may already be aware of these messages and confidently use them to guide yourself. The more you have successfully followed your intuitive guidance in the past, the more likely it is that you will be comfortable using it again, even if you don't know the source of your awareness. Even if using your intuition is new to you, you can learn how to recognize and interpret the messages.

Your early life experiences can make you particularly susceptible to certain kinds of information that exists below the threshold of your awareness. If you grew up on a farm or ranch, you may "know" about impending weather changes without consulting the official forecast. If you grew up in a family where alcohol was abused, you may "know" when someone has been drinking when no signs are visible to a casual observer. If you grew up with unpredictable outbursts of rage, you may be particularly aware of others' moods and needs. Start to pay attention to your body's wisdom. When you feel sensations shift for no apparent reason, take a quiet moment to reflect on what could be happening outside yourself that you might be reacting to. Then go back over recent thoughts and situations that might have affected you. The more frequently you study these signals and speculate on their meaning, the more comfortable you will become in interpreting them. Remember, the signals are probably not logical. The connections may even seem silly or decidedly far-fetched, but they may be useful nonetheless.

Intuitive knowing may protect you from danger or provide needed wisdom when you are at the end of your resources. You may find that you use it as a source of guidance in everyday situations. You may experience this knowing as a deep inner knowing or as a still small voice. It may seem to come from outside you, and perhaps it does. Nobody knows for certain. Whatever its source, it can be a valuable tool to help you search for your own truth.

Some individuals become so adept at recognizing and trusting their intuitive guidance that they make major life decisions based on gut feelings or hunches. In *The Soul of a Business: Managing for Profit and the Common Good*, Tom Chappell describes in detail how he uses intuition in product development at Tom's of Maine (1993). Others work for years to learn to interpret and trust this information source. If you want to develop your own intuitive awareness, it is sometimes helpful to talk to supportive friends about what you are doing. The members of Elizabeth's team learned about the inner signals they were ignoring once Elizabeth shared her signals with them. Being with someone who supports you in making intuitive judgments helps, too. David Neenan, president of The Neenan Company, a rapidly growing, innovative contracting firm in Colorado, encouraged his management team to follow their own intuition. When his general manager reluctantly terminated the employment of a foreman he had hired, saying that he had been afraid it would not work out, David asked him why. The general manager reported that he had a funny feeling about the foreman when he first hired him, but that he thought that the guy deserved a chance anyway. David encouraged his general manager to honor feelings like that in the future and search until he found employees he really felt comfortable hiring.

Of course, intuition is only part of the picture. You certainly will want your logical mind to examine your intuitive conclusions. When both parts of your mind are in agreement, you will feel the most confidence with your decisions. You are probably well trained in logical problem solving, but in some situations your logical mind misses important information that your intuition could supply, if you were open to receiving it. If your intuitive abilities are underdeveloped, you may want to spend time and attention learning to use them effectively.

Developing Your Intuition

1. Learn to pay attention to your own feelings and sensations. They may signal the emergence of intuitive information. In order to open yourself up to experiencing your intuition, you may need to learn to quiet the jumble of thoughts that are constantly surging through your mind.

2. Practice simple focusing techniques to quiet yourself. You may find that sitting quietly in a natural setting is helpful. Saying a simply phrase over and over again (a mantra) in your mind can also help you focus. There are many fine books and tapes available to help you learn these skills. I recommend *How to Meditate* by Lawrence LeShan (1974), *The Relaxation Response* by Herbert Benson (1975), *Wherever You Go, There You Are* by Jon Kabat Zinn (1994), and *Buddha's Little Instruction Book* by Jack Kornfield (1994).

3. Listen to yourself speak. Your language may provide clues. When you say someone is a pain in the neck, do you know what you mean? When you say (or think) that someone makes you sick, there is usually a reason for that statement.

4. Keep a record of your dreams. Even tiny fragments of dreams can give you clues to hidden information. Keep writing materials next to your bed, and record your memories as soon as you awaken, before you do anything else. Dreams fade quickly.

5. Honor your hunches, gut feelings, and the quiet inner voice that suggests that you need to take an unexpected direction. Pay attention to them and think about them. Ask questions. Calibrate your responses until you develop confidence in your intuitive abilities.

6. If you would like to learn a lot more about this fascinating subject, which takes truth-telling into different dimensions, contact The Intuition Network for their listings of publications, computer conferences, seminars, and study groups (see Appendix 1).

References

Benson, H. *The Relaxation Response.* New York: Morrow, 1975.

Chappell, T. *The Soul of a Business: Managing for Profit and the Common Good.* New York: Bantam Books, 1993.

Kabat-Zinn, J. *Wherever You Go, There You Are.* New York: Hyperion, 1994.

Kornfield, J. *Buddha's Little Instruction Book.* New York: Bantam Books, 1994.

LeShan, L. L. *How to Meditate: A Guide to Self-Discovery.* Boston: G. K. Hall, 1974.

CHAPTER

14

The Truth Will Set You Free, but First It May Make You Mad!

Pete reluctantly agreed to hire another consultant to help his executive team clarify what was causing several key professionals to consider resigning from his agency. When several problems were identified, including Pete's inconsistent leadership style, he courageously suggested that the group first focus on his leadership. It was difficult for him to hear the negative feedback, but as he listened and responded, the team members' animosity changed to offers of help and support.

Pete had watched as the new consultant listed the areas his associates on the executive team had identified as problems needing attention in order for the team to function effectively. He knew that dissension was threatening the survival of the team. This meeting was a final attempt to salvage the situation. Pete recognized that the truth had to be told, but he felt frustrated and angry each time his name was written on the newsprint. "Anger at Pete," "Pete's management style," "unclear directions," "inadequate leadership" all appeared on the list, along with "time pressure, stress, and poor communication."

Pete *already* knew there were problems on the team. There had been problems with the team when he had accepted the job as director of the agency a year ago. The twice-monthly meetings with the last consultant had usually turned into gripe sessions, ending with everyone feeling frustrated. This inherited mess had gotten worse with each passing month, and Pete knew he did not have the skills to solve the problem. He did not even really know what the problem was. Now two of his three fellow attorneys were threatening to resign if things did not improve. His team seemed to be in agreement, though. The three accountants, the office manager, and the other three attorneys had all listed similar issues.

When the consultant asked the team to prioritize the issues, Pete got a firm grip on his anger and decided to get the worst over with. He said, "Since so many of the problems seem to be related to my leadership, let's start with that." The team breathed a collective sigh of relief, since the not-so-secret purpose of the meeting had been to address just that issue. Expecting to be the scapegoat one more time, and not really expecting the consultant to be of any particular help, Pete thought to himself, "If I could only understand what they want, perhaps then I could figure out how to give it to them."

The consultant asked team members to spell out some of the specific incidents that were bothering them. One of the attorneys was angry about his job evaluation; another was angry because each time he tried to discuss a case with Pete, Pete would be distracted by another issue, and the discussion would never be completed. Two of the accountants agreed that Pete did not acknowledge their heroic efforts to manage an admittedly impossible work load. The office manager was upset because Pete was so far behind on his paperwork that every time she needed him to review a decision, the necessary information got lost on his desk.

Each time Pete heard a complaint, he wanted to counter it with an explanation of his behavior. He was sure that they had no idea what kind of pressure he was experiencing from the board and the CEO to get the agency into shape; and the powers that be also wanted him to take on an enormous new project. (Pete actually wished that he could devote most of his time to the new project and forget the day-to-day hassles.) The consultant coached Pete to repeat back to each team member his understanding of what he had just said, and to ask each person only questions that would help clarify the problems that person was experiencing. Pete had a difficult time holding his anger in check and not responding defensively, but he managed. His restraint was rewarded.

Pete was amazed at the change that came over the team members as he listened to them and asked questions only to further his understanding of their perceptions. When he made no attempt to correct or challenge them, they visibly relaxed. They actually looked at him instead of averting their eyes. Three of them even smiled after a while. This was not turning out nearly as badly as he had expected it to. He was even beginning to understand the common themes in their stories.

When he was given the opportunity to respond to what he had heard, he found that he no longer wanted to defend his behavior. Instead he was somehow able to respond with a deeper truth. He admitted that he often felt unsure of himself and that he did not know much about being a leader. He described how difficult it was for him to evaluate another person, especially without stepping on that person's toes (or feelings). He also acknowledged that the hectic way he operated was a result of his attempt to fix all the problems that were brought to his attention. He expressed his dilemma by saying he wished he knew how to be a leader without being forced to become a parent.

The truthful dialogue had begun. Team members responded that they did not want him to solve problems for them; they wanted him to understand what their problems were. Pete's anxiety diminished when he understood that they would be satisfied if he would only listen to them the way he had been listening to them for the past hour. He began to see that his team members were all highly skilled professionals and only wanted his support, direction, and encouragement to do their work themselves. They were even enthusiastic about helping him with some of the challenges he was facing.

This meeting left everyone feeling cautiously optimistic. Over the next several weeks Pete made a determined effort to actively listen to the members of his team. Gradually they seemed to be developing more trust in his leadership. Pete's model of courage and adaptability inspired the other team members to examine their own behaviors individually and as a group. The situation improved, but problems kept recurring. Whenever the pressure grew too great, they all tended to revert to their former behaviors.

In their twice-monthly meetings with the new consultant the complaints continued. "Pete forgot to give feedback." "Pete tried to solve every problem they told him about." "Pete was overcritical and overcontrolling." "Pete was absent when he was needed."

One important change was permanent. During each meeting Pete listened carefully and respectfully to every statement, and the members of his team listened too. As it became safer to tell the truth, the level of trust increased. Over the next eighteen months all the members of the agency began to discuss their own responsibility for gossiping about problems instead of immediately attempting to correct them.

They decided that they needed to discuss any problem with the appropriate person at the first available opportunity. They learned to discuss formerly taboo topics such as ongoing conflict between team members, and they became adept at examining how they functioned together as a team. Pete was encouraged to focus on enhancing relationships with the larger organization and the community. As they supported Pete, it became easier for him to argue for the extra personnel the agency needed to handle the workload.

Twenty-one months after the first meeting, the discussion turned to how the executives could introduce and perpetuate their healthy team structure with the new members of the expanding agency. They were successful, and when the agency doubled its professional staff, they maintained the atmosphere of trust and truth-telling. Pete was able to spend much of his time doing the developmental work he enjoyed most, and his executive team kept the work flowing smoothly. Two years later they discontinued the quarterly meetings with me, their consultant.

Creating an Atmosphere That Encourages Trust and Truth-Telling

The key ingredient in turning around Pete's agency was his willingness to set aside his own anger and defensiveness long enough to really hear what others were saying. At first Pete needed coaching and support to learn to truly listen to his team, but when he discovered how powerfully he affected others by just listening to them, he wanted to continue to use this skill.

Perhaps the greatest gift you can give to another person is your full attention. Everyone wants to be heard and understood, and in our fast-paced and competitive world we rarely experience this luxury. Wanting to be acknowledged, wanting to be seen and heard, reflects one of our most basic needs as human beings. In order to live at all when we first came into the world we needed love and attention from others. This need never disappears!

At first, Pete, like most of us, was more concerned with being seen and heard than in hearing others. Although most adults no longer need others to care for their physical needs, the emotional need for caring recognition is always with us. We all learn many tricks or defensive routines to avoid feeling the pain associated with not being accepted with love. Pete's impulses to defend himself came from his normal need to protect himself from feeling the hurt of not being accepted. When he was able to switch his attention to listening to others, he allowed them to experience the caring acceptance they needed. For most of us, just experiencing being heard helps us feel loved.

When someone hears you, you assume that he or she cares about you. When this happens over and over again, you begin to feel safe. After all, if you know that person cares about you, you expect him or her to be interested in your well-being. If you feel safe, you begin to trust others, and your need to defend yourself from them diminishes. It becomes easier to tell the truth when you feel safe, and when you no longer need to defend yourself it becomes easier to listen to and accept others.

Somebody needs to go first! Shifting from a cycle of accusation and defensiveness to one of listening and acceptance is risky. After all, if you let down your defenses, you are vulnerable. The real question becomes, what are you vulnerable to? What terrible thing do you expect to happen if you don't defend yourself? *Usually the terrible thing you fear has already happened to you many times.* Someone rejects you, and you do not like it. In extreme situations you may even have felt sick, bad, stupid, or crazy when this occurred, but usually the negative feeling is a temporary discomfort. Pete recognized this and was able to take the risk of going first.

Being willing to listen is the first step. Learning to listen skillfully is the next challenge. Skillful listening requires that you attend to both the content and the context of a communication. In a sense it is like listening to both the words and the melody of a song simultaneously.

The first step is to focus attention on the person who is speaking to you and just listen to the words that are being spoken. Sometimes your own emotional responses will get in your way. If you feel attacked by the speaker's words, you may keep thinking of things to say to defend yourself. Then you lose track of what the other person is saying to you. If you can refocus on listening until you are sure that you thoroughly understand the speaker, you may discover how much you miss by responding defensively.

If you are a very intense, impatient person, you may also find yourself feeling bored and angry about how long it takes someone who speaks more slowly to express themselves fully. You may be able to stay involved more easily by repeatedly checking your understanding of the speaker's statements.

Once you learn to listen to the ideas that are being communicated (the words of the song), your next challenge is to learn to understand the emotions that are being expressed along with the spoken words (the music). Emotions are expressed by facial expressions, by voice tone, pitch, and tempo, and by body posture and gestures. You have emotional responses to all these signals, even when you are not conscious of what the speaker did to trigger them. When you notice that you are having an emotional response, be alert for the emotions being expressed by the speaker.

Emotions usually become the background or context of a communication and may convey more truthful information than words do. People feel understood when you deliberately use words to acknowledge their emotions. Saying, "I can hear how angry you feel" can change a speaker's anger into immense relief. When someone feels understood, the intensity of their emotions usually diminishes.

As you become a better listener, others are likely to feel more comfortable sharing important information with you. This is a critical step for creating an atmosphere of trust in any group of people. Pete did not have many listening skills at first; he learned them along the way. You can learn to listen, too. Becoming a nondefensive, skilled, and willing listener can change the quality of all your relationships.

Learning to Listen

1.   Make a commitment to yourself to listen until the other person has finished communicating. Interrupt only to ask them to clarify what they are telling you. Hold your own thoughts and responses until they are finished.

2.   Listen to the words that are being said and to the emotional tone that accompanies the words. Emotions may be expressed through tone of voice, volume (loud or soft), the pace of words (fast or slow), and the facial expression and body position of the speaker.

3.   When a pause occurs, or when you have heard as much as you can manage to keep track of at one time, tell the speaker what you understand about what they have said. Either repeat or paraphrase their words, and use your own words to describe their emotions. You may need to interrupt and say something like "Let me check my understanding so far. You are angry because I did not keep our appointment and did not let you know in advance. You did not have a chance to make other plans." *Be sure to repeat the words the speaker has used!* Listeners who simply say, "I understand," may have missed something important.

4.   When the speaker seems to have finished, ask, "Is there anything else?" If there is something else, continue to listen and paraphrase what you hear. Often the "something else" is the emotion associated with the words. Some people do not feel

heard unless the listener displays an emotional intensity similar to their own. One way to express your understanding is by matching the loudness or softness of your own words to those of the speaker.

5.   When the speaker has finished, summarize everything the person has said. Then, if you can, try to step into that person's shoes and empathize with his or her position: "If I had experienced what you did, I'm sure I would have felt similarly."

6.   After you are finished listening, decide whether this would be a good time to share your own views. Often it is useful to wait until another time. If you are trying to mend a difficult situation, you may need to just listen several times before the other person is ready to hear you.

7.   Seek balance. No relationship, business or personal, can thrive if one person always listens and is never heard. Each person needs to balance hearing others and being heard.

CHAPTER

15

Get the Information You Need Without Being Gullible or Paranoid

A group of frustrated business owners concluded that "candidates for jobs lie up a storm." Elaine, the president of a temporary staffing agency, agreed, adding that it is hard for people who are "scrambling to try to get decent positions" to be completely truthful about their qualifications. Yet the reputation of her company depends upon creating a good match between the candidate and the prospective employer. She believes it is the job of the interviewer to help candidates tell the truth about themselves so they can be placed where they are most likely to be successful.

Elaine Demery, president of Nelson, Coulson and Associates, Inc., knows that job candidates are not always in a good position to assess the personal qualities that would allow them to succeed in many of the jobs they seek. She reports that "in a highly competitive job market, candidates sometimes exaggerate their strengths." Yet she believes that most do not deliberately lie; instead "they want very much to be the person you're looking for," so they "tell you what they think you want to hear."

In a world where there are a hundred candidates for every good job, where attorneys and paralegals are doing secretarial work in law firms and where former middle managers with master's degrees are driving taxicabs and serving pizzas, she does not find exaggeration by job candidates at all surprising. It is simply a reflection of human nature. "Candidates *have to* make a living to support themselves or others. They need to get the best possible job at the best possible rate."

Prospective employers want to believe what candidates tell them. Their businesses need help, and they usually need help immediately. Elaine observes, "Everyone wants so much for it to work" that unskilled interviewers frequently ask questions that are "basically leading that candidate to tell them what they want to hear." Interviewers may not even know how to ask the questions that will get them the information they need.

Elaine believes that the job interviewing process becomes so convoluted that it is easy for both potential employers and job candidates to deceive themselves about the suitability of a match. At an interview you are always putting your best foot forward," she said. "Three months later, you may have totally different perceptions. There is a lot of disillusionment."

She knows how costly hiring mistakes can be, especially for smaller companies with ten or fewer employees. One mismatched employee who does not fit in or cannot do the job that is needed can cause a major disruption in the business. She knows that both prospective employers and prospective employees must be helped to communicate effectively. Her goal is to move all her clients beyond their mutual self-deception and help make placements that work.

Elaine knows personally how easy it is to deceive herself. As an employer, she admits that she is prone to falling into the same traps that she now tries to help others avoid. She admitted, "I thought I was a good communicator, and I found out I wasn't. I would be totally surprised when I learned what my employees thought I wanted."

Nelson, Coulson has twenty employees, and Elaine was frustrated because a series of employees at the front desk lasted only nine to fourteen months each in that position. They would start out just fine, and after a while things would deteriorate. As she reflected on why she was so appreciative and happy when they started and became so dissatisfied later, she realized that "as time went by, I would take them for granted. I did not remember to tell them the wonderful things I was thinking about them. Now when I notice an employee doing something great, I am learning to tell him or her on the spot, 'That was fabulous, you did a great job,' or 'I think you handled that beautifully.' Very open communication skills are important."

After years of experience, she is convinced that the most important factor in placing nontechnical employees in suitable positions is a correct personality match between the candidate and the position. It helps the communication flow naturally. Job skills are secondary. "If there is a good personality match and a 75 percent adequate skill level, the other 25 percent will be forgiven. A person who can handle all the work but is not a good personality match simply doesn't fit and won't work out." The problem has been that neither the employer nor the candidate may have the skills to recognize what makes a good personality match.

Creating a good fit between the candidate and the job depends on knowing what the job is really like. If her people just ask the employer to provide a description of the skills required to perform a particular job, they will not get all the necessary information. Elaine has trained her staff to ask questions about a variety of other factors that she believes are critical for creating a successful match. She has found that the more specific the questions they ask, the more likely it is that the potential employer will give an accurate and truthful description of the position.

When interviewing a prospective employer, Nelson, Coulson staff members learn about the physical working environment. Is the job done in a closed private office or in a noisy open area where many people share the space? They learn how a particular employer measures success on the job. Does the employer want someone who follows instructions exactly or someone who is more creative? Does the employer value analytical skills over friendliness or vice versa? Staff members visit prospective job sites to develop descriptions of the traits a candidate needs in order to be successful at that particular job.

Nelson, Coulson provides temporary staffing for large and small companies. Elaine measures her success by how satisfied employers are with a candidate. She knows companies are happy when they keep some of her temporary placements for years. Another sign of success is that the candidates she has placed are eventually hired by the companies as regular employees. Loyal clients have made Nelson, Coulson and Associates, Inc. one of the largest women-owned businesses in Colorado.

Encouraging Truth-Telling in Interviews

Elaine believes, "People basically want to get along, feel secure, do a good job, and be appreciated." To ensure such an outcome, her company uses an interviewing system that allows and encourages candidates to tell the truth about what they are really like and what they need to be successful in a job. Instead of interviewing candidates for specific jobs, staff members at Nelson, Coulson interview candidates to learn their strengths and preferences. They try to ease the pressure on candidates by assuring them, "We have so many different opportunities. We want to make sure we get the right one for you."

Counselors refer to a list of about twenty different personality traits during the interview. First candidates identify their own personality traits by taking a written survey during which they choose scenarios in which they would feel either comfortable or uncomfortable. Then they are given the opportunity, through answering more questions, to describe how they have demonstrated those traits in previous jobs. Instead of asking candidates yes or no questions such as "Are you organized?" candidates are presented with a series of common business challenges and asked to describe how they have managed similar situations in the past.

When Elaine interviewed me as a potential job candidate, she asked, "In your prior job at ABC Company, please give me a specific example of how you made choices about priorities when you had many tasks to do at the same time."

Elaine wants to discover what characteristics are most important, both for the employer and for the candidate. She knows when anyone is presented with a list of positive personality traits and skills, most people will identify with all the characteristics. What employer wouldn't want someone who is creative, analytical, people oriented, detail oriented, and organized? What candidate wouldn't think to themselves, "I could do that" (be people oriented, detail oriented, organized, analytical, and creative) and say so to an interviewer?

She explains that although we all have some of each of these characteristics, Nelson, Coulson is screening for only those traits that are most important for a candidate's success in a particular job. Once her staff identifies which are the top five qualities needed by an employer for a particular job and which are the top five qualities that describe a candidate, they can make effective matches. The critical factor is getting accurate information by asking performance-based questions, and with the right kind of question it is easier for everyone involved to tell the truth.

Getting Truthful Information to Make a Decision

Although you may not be seeking employment or looking for an employee, every time you make a major decision, such as purchasing or choosing on project over another, you want accurate information to help you make a good choice. When the people from whom you seek the information have a strong personal interest in the outcome of your decision, the situation can get sticky. You want to trust what they are saying, but you fear that they may be "lying up a storm" in order to get your cooperation, approval, or money.

When faced with this dilemma, some people go to extremes. You may know people (or maybe you're like this yourself) who get so excited about the prospect of starting a new project or purchasing a new car that they throw caution to the wind, accept all promises at face value, and believe that everything will be just fine. Sometimes everything is just fine, but, unfortunately, there are often unpleasant surprises after the commitment has been made.

You may know others who are so cautious that they spend months gathering every scrap of information that might be helpful in making an important decision. They take so long to decide that they miss out on opportunities to take timely actions that would benefit them.

Most of us try to find a middle course between the two extremes. We do not want to be either gullible or paranoid; we want to find a way to get the information we need to make informed decisions. If you want to avoid being gullible, it helps to understand your own objectives and vulnerabilities given your situation. If you want to avoid being paranoid, it helps to understand what motivates the others in the situation, and to be willing to help them achieve their objectives. You should also be able to use communication skills to search for and negotiate a win-win outcome for everyone concerned.

It is very important to clearly understand your own objectives before you enter into agreements with others. If you need a specific job completed by a specific time within a specific budget, clarify what you need before you begin to search for the help you want. The project can be as simple as hiring a teenager to cut your lawn, or as complex as hiring architects and contractors to build a new building for you. If a coworker wants you to help him meet a deadline, think carefully about how much time you can spare and still keep your other commitments before you agree to his request.

Learning to recognize your own vulnerabilities will help you avoid repeating situations in which you think you are about to get what you want and find yourself disappointed once again. One way to do this is to think about what you were trying to accomplish just before you realized that "it" had happened again. "It" is different for everyone. "It" may be losing money, ending a promising relationship, having to do a lot of extra work, or missing an opportunity.

Janet was vulnerable because she wanted everyone to like her. She was always there to help when someone needed a rush job done. She would stay late at the office and finish the job no matter what activities she had planned for herself. She kept hoping that someone would recognize her heroic efforts, but no one did. In fact, they did not even say thank you. Instead everyone began to assume that she would take care of all emergencies. She began to feel like a victim instead of a hero. (Review Chapter 4 for a description of the victim position.)

If you feel like you are getting stuck in a negative, unproductive role like Janet's, identify what you are trying to accomplish by acting the way you do. Then plan a new strategy to get what you need. When Janet finally understood that people did not like her any more because she did extra work, she decided to stop staying late and instead spend more time with friends who already liked her. As she relaxed more, others seemed to become friendlier at work. Think about what you need to do to get out of your own trap. Sometimes simply asking for what you really want will solve the problem.

Getting more information can help you avoid feeling paranoid about someone else's intentions. Finding out as much as you can about the other person's needs in the situation will help you begin to establish trust with that person. The simplest way to do this is to ask specific questions about what is important to the other person.

Tricia's supervisor set the stage for mutual trust by asking what the company could do to make it worth her while to assist at a company retreat. Tricia, a single parent, promptly replied that she would really appreciate flexible scheduling so that she could attend her children's school programs.

If you take a cooperative attitude and maintain your own boundaries, you will be less likely to make decisions you will regret. If you feel pressured by someone who wants you to do something that you really don't want to do, try to think about other ways to help that person get what he or she needs. Do your best to form an alliance with the other person to reach a common objective.

When Phillip's service club president asked him to coordinate a complex time-consuming project, he felt a great deal of pressure to accept the assignment. Philip knew he did not have enough time or interest to do a good job on the project, but he almost said yes anyway. Instead he thought about it and agreed to take on a small but important piece of the project and suggested someone else he thought would make a great project manager.

Sandra, who agreed to coordinate the project, was candid about her own objectives in the situation. She explained to the club president, "I'm new in the area, and I think that doing this project will be a great showcase for my skills. I hope that when I demonstrate how competent I am, other members will refer clients to me."

The club president was delighted. He needed the job done and was in a position to help Sandra get the clients she needed. He took every possible opportunity to call attention to her achievements when she helped the club exceed its goals. Sandra soon had all the business she could manage.

At other times you may feel paranoid because a situation is confusing and you don't really understand why. It may be that someone's words may not match their body posture or tone of voice. This kind of incongruent communication is common. If you feel confused, admit it, and ask for clarification.

When Irene asked Jack to write an article for the company newsletter, he shrugged and said, "Sure, I'll try to get around to it soon." Irene was not sure whether or not he had agreed to write the article, so she commented that he did not seem enthusiastic about doing it. Jack admitted that he really didn't want to but felt he should. Irene said that she could find someone else to do it, and he smiled with relief and thanked her for letting him off the hook.

You may also begin to feel uncomfortable when you are not getting the information you need during a conversation, even though someone appears to be politely answering your questions. You may be tempted to accept what they say just to avoid appearing dumb or impolite (your vulnerabilities). This sometimes happens when you are trying to thread your way through a bureaucracy or any situation where you are dealing with someone who also wants to avoid appearing dumb or impolite.

It is easy to lose your place in a conversation. Sometimes someone gives an answer that is slightly different from what was called for by the question asked. You need to keep track of what your question was. It is surprisingly easy to forget it and just continue on the conversation as if you have been given the information you requested. Stay alert. It may seem impolite to ask your question again, but do it anyway. It may even be useful to try a different approach. Don't give up.

Ralph needed to purchase a new copy machine. The sales representative assured him that the one he was interested in was one of the best models available in Ralph's price range. When Ralph asked for the cost per copy, the sales representative told him it was very low. This was a general answer, but it was not a specific answer to Ralph's question. He recognized that he did not yet have the information he needed, so he asked the representative to compute the cost per copy based on the estimated life and replacement costs of the machine's components. The representative soon found him a specification sheet that gave Ralph the information he needed.

These suggestions should help you create truthful sharing of information with most people, although, in some situations, people will tell you what they think you want to hear, and would consider it rude to do otherwise. Other people may have their own hidden reasons to avoid giving you the information you want. Occasionally you will come across a con artist who intends to treat you dishonestly. Just remember that when something sounds too good to be true, it probably is. Be extra cautious when you are pressured to make a quick decision with insufficient information.

How to Minimize Paranoia and Avoid Gullibility

When you find yourself having to engage in negotiations, whether it involves purchasing equipment, hiring a firm to provide a service, or dealing with a superior to resolve a work-related issue, you should have a clear strategy for approaching the interaction. The following points provide some guidance.

1. Know what you want. Get very clear about your objectives before you enter into agreements with others.

2. Learn to recognize your own vulnerabilities and use extra time and attention to carefully consider all your options when you know you may not be thinking clearly.

3. Find out as much as you can about the other person's needs in the situation. Ask specific questions to learn what is important to that person.

4. Think about ways in which you might be able to help the other person get what he or she needs.

5. Be candid about your own objectives in the situation.

6. Do your best to form alliances with others to reach common objectives.

7. Pay attention to the actual words that the other person is saying and to the body language that accompanies them. If you feel confused, admit it and ask for clarification.

8. Notice whether on not you are getting the information you need during the course of the interaction. If you are not getting what you need to know, try a different approach. Don't give up.

9. Remember that when something sounds too good to be true, it probably is. Be extra cautious when you are pressured to make a quick decision with insufficient information.

CHAPTER

16

Ask Questions with Grace and Skill

David, a young engineer and team leader at a major electronics firm, used the information he learned at a team development workshop to help his team produce spectacular results. When he was asked to describe his methods at a briefing session for senior management, David first asked questions to get a sense of what he could contribute to their discussion. They were surprised to discover that he was asking about important issues they had not really addressed. Within a year, David became a valued in-house consultant for his company.

"Prior to my program, our production was at a very poor quality level, and we were constantly under enormous stress," David recalled. He instituted the program after attending an intensive workshop that emphasized the value of telling the truth and accepting personal responsibility for the results he created. When he acknowledged responsibility for "how I contributed to the stress level," and shared this information with others, he started to transform his career.

David returned to work full of new ideas about how to improve productivity on a very troublesome product. His new insight and clarity helped him convince the production manager to allow him to test his ideas immediately. The results were remarkable. The computer print-head the team produced improved in quality so dramatically that instead of failing 25 percent of the time, it became almost defect free within two months. In the same time period production costs dropped an astonishing 65 percent.

Amazed by the power of helping his 35-member group to establish a purpose for the team and to learn to follow a set of agreements about how to relate to each other, David watched them make, and then regularly exceed their goals. When the excitement spread to the remainder of the 115-member production team, David realized that helping a work team create synergy could make an enormous impact within the organization. He was also enjoying himself. "Creating the team that did this was one of the most gratifying, fun, and rewarding experiences I have ever had," he said.

In David's company, operating with integrity was one of the guiding principles. Each year each person in the company was required to reaffirm this principle: "We conduct our business with uncompromising integrity." The team building tools he was teaching provided a blueprint for expanding the use of this principle into new areas. His spectacular results earned him the right to present his ideas to higher management. He wanted the opportunity to help other teams improve their results by teaching them to operate more effectively with each other.

Attending a meeting to explain his program to managers several levels above himself, David found he had an opportunity to use his new skills in a different arena. He did not fully understand all of the issues being discussed, so instead of sitting quietly and trying to figure things out or pretending that he understood everything, he started to question everything he did not understand. He knew that he could not effectively serve this new group if he was not clear about what they needed. Borrowing techniques he had practiced with his own team, he made certain that his questions acknowledged his own responsibility for his lack of information.

As David admitted that he did not fully understand what this management group was discussing, he noticed with surprise that several of the senior managers also admitted their confusion! Some of the senior managers reassured him that they were responsible for the lack of clarity in the meeting. The managers were impressed with David's courage and clarity. Their meeting was far more productive because his questions had highlighted some problem areas that were not being addressed.

David asked questions without challenging anyone's competence or pet theories. Without coming across as intrusive or threatening, he enhanced group members' ability to communicate more productively. He did not tell them what was or was not true; he did not have that information himself. He created an opportunity for them to do their own work more effectively, and to discover the truth for themselves.

David negotiated an in-house consulting job with the company, and within a few months he had set up over forty additional teams and taught a dozen workshops on the concepts he was using. He focused on teaching members of these groups to be "more effective, more productive, and to enjoy their jobs more." All of the teams dramatically increased both the quality and efficiency of production, and many set records that had previously been unthinkable. The product improvement achieved by one team's contribution was so dramatic that the company received a very prestigious industrial achievement award.

Summarizing his work, David wrote, "I have made major changes in myself, and I feel I have added tremendous value to those I have worked with." A year later he left the company and became an independent consultant, teaching productivity enhancement classes to many other groups throughout the United States. David found this work was less satisfying because, for him, getting a team started was not as much fun as helping a team work through the entire process and produce results.

After "getting a taste of how other companies were managed" and working at another company for two and a half years, David realized how fortunate he had been at the original company. Six years later he returned to them as a research and development project manager. Today he supervises the work of ten Ph.D.'s and is thrilled to be back in an environment where "people are mentored and earn their way up by creating results." He is relieved to be away from the authoritarian structures and political infighting he encountered in other companies. After a recent performance review, he reports with pleasure, "My team says that I really listen to them."

The Right Questions Invite Thoughtful and Truthful Answers

David does more than just listen to his team. Over the years he has developed a strategy of asking penetrating questions that almost force people to think through situations in depth. Then he listens very carefully to their responses. He believes that people search for the truth and then share it with him because of two important factors. First, his "motive is pure"; he is interested in getting the job done and creating a winning situation for the people he is working with; he is not interested in manipulating them. Second, he goes to great pains to make certain that others never feel threatened or put down by his questions.

David explained: "I have developed a knack for asking questions that nobody else would ask. Sometimes these questions are quite confrontational. I ask questions in order to get very clear about what is happening. I believe that people do things and don't understand why [they do those things]. I try to figure out why these people are doing what they do. Then I ask a question that helps them understand their own motives. When they get clear, they know what to do next. They often tell me that they are glad I asked the question."

David wants to make it safe for the people he works with to tell the truth. He never blames anyone else for a problem or a miscommunication. If there is any blame, he assumes it himself by the way he asks his questions. He demonstrates taking responsibility for learning by modeling that responsibility for others.

He is likely to preface a question with a disarming statement such as

- "I'm really confused here."
- "I'm sorry, would you mind going over that again?"
- "I must have heard this wrong before."
- "I must have really screwed up."

Management trainer Abe Wagner refers to these disarming statements as "face-saving devices" (Wagner and Wagner 1997). By giving people excuses for inappropriate behavior or unclear communication, you avoid causing them embarrassment.

David believes that taking this responsibility on yourself leads everyone to assume personal responsibility for his or her own work. He has observed that whenever he offers to assume blame for a problem, others are quick to argue that they are responsible for the problem themselves. David described the process: "Their fear that someone will see something they thought was hidden diminishes, and they acknowledge their own shortcomings. They don't spend all their energy defending their turf. Instead they get almost jealous of the positive response I get when I take responsibility for my own lack of understanding. They want some of that, too."

David is still amazed at the amount of energy people in business use to defend themselves: "Once you do it [tell the truth about your own shortcomings], it works so well it becomes a part of your M.O. I don't think about it anymore—it has become a part of me." David is very clear that this is not just a technique. "If you are honest and it comes from your heart, they know it. People's barriers go down, and they tell the truth."

Even when someone has made an error, and both David and the guilty party know it, David does his best to make it easier for the other person to accept his or her own mistakes. In one touchy situation David told another manager, "Gee, I'm usually the one that misses all that stuff. It's nice to know someone else does it, too." For David, this statement is true. He is aware of times he has made mistakes, and he is not afraid to let others know this truth about himself. This "appropriate self-disclosure" also makes it easier for others to accept constructive advice (Wagner and Wagner 1997).

David has discovered a principal of leadership espoused in the ancient Chinese book of practical wisdom, the *Tao Te Ching* (Mitchell 1988): "By not dominating, the Master leads." He knows what he intends to accomplish, but he is willing to be responsive to others before asking for their cooperation. "I believe people have difficulty getting into a meaningful dialogue because they come with different expectations," David noted.

"I have found that at first you have to be willing to forgo your own agenda and focus on their agenda. After doing this a few times, they seem to go out of their way to help you." David's focus on supporting and mentoring others has allowed him to become an exceptionally effective leader—and he loves his work.

David also uses his own mistakes as an opportunity to examine and improve his own skills. When a dialogue is unproductive, he questions himself: He asks, "What is going on here? What am I doing that isn't helping?" Often he finds that the problem is that he has become distracted and is not giving his full attention to the situation. "Sometimes my body language is messed up, and I look like I am going away," he admitted. "I turn straight to them, say 'Excuse me, I was distracted,' and give them my full attention. I consider it a tremendous acknowledgment when they really open up, tell the truth, and walk away happy."

Developing Skills in Asking Questions

1. Gather as much information as you can about a situation by careful observation. This includes listening to the topics that are discussed and noticing those that are not discussed. It also includes paying attention to nonverbal clues—posture, relative power positions of the people present in the situation, even furniture placement and seating arrangements.

2. Think about what additional information you need to better understand the situation. Look for the missing pieces.

3. Use your intuition. What is your hunch or guess about what is going on? What do you wish you knew?

4. Before you ask any questions, remind yourself that the person you want to question is very important. It is especially

useful to remember this if you are in a senior position to that person. It helps you avoid any unconsciously condescending behavior.

5. Ask questions only when you are truly unsure of what the answers will be, and when you are willing to listen carefully to the answers that are presented to you. A common reason to ask a question when you are already sure of the answer is to catch someone else doing something wrong. If you do this, others will sense it and feel resentful or put down even if you think you are being subtle.

6. Borrow some of David's language, and learn to verbally disarm yourself. Practice a few of David's expressions, even if they seem a little uncomfortable at first.

7. Be willing to be vulnerable. Take responsibility for your own mistakes or lack of information. In this situation, saving face (your own) is not nearly as important as helping others save face!

8. Once you ask your question, LISTEN TO THE ANSWER! Give it your full attention. Ask clarifying questions only if you cannot understand the answer you are hearing. Otherwise, wait until the answer is complete before you comment on it.

9. Tell the other person that you appreciate his or her competence and good will.

10. If you feel attacked or challenged by the answer to one of your questions, do not defend yourself. Respond with your understanding of what was said, and ask if your understanding is accurate.

11. Keep asking questions until you are sure you understand what you need to know about the situation, and as long as others are willing to respond to you.

12. After you fully understand the other person's communication, decide if you need to clarify or discuss the reasons for your actions. It might be best to delay the discussion until a later time.

References

Mitchell, S., trans. *Tao Te Ching: A New English Version.* New York: Harper and Row, 1988.

Wagner, A., and D. Wagner. *The Diversity Formula.* London: The Industrial Society of London, 1997.

CHAPTER

17

Tell Your Truth with Compassion for Yourself and Others

Valerie struggled with herself about how to inform her client that she suspected he was using drugs. As she prepared him for job interviews, she started to think that other interviewers might notice the subtle symptoms and mannerisms she had observed in him. She carefully examined her own internal conversation and her fear of alienating her client. Her commitment to her own integrity helped her find an appropriate way to take the necessary risk while continuing to support her client.

Valerie noticed that the pupils of her client's eyes were dilated. She had noticed the same thing in an earlier session and said nothing, but now she was even more concerned. She strongly suspected that he was using drugs. What was her responsibility in this situation? Her client, Tim, was a pleasant enough young man, and he had worked hard to make use of her coaching. As a recent college graduate with excellent technical skills, but very poor relationship and interviewing skills, he definitely needed her help.

The situation was even more complex because Tim's father was paying for his coaching. Valerie was concerned that Tim's commitment to the coaching process might be compromised because he was not paying for her services. She was very afraid that if she mentioned her suspicions to Tim, she would alienate him. If he actually was using drugs, she thought he would probably lie and say he was not. If her suspicion was incorrect, he would probably be insulted. No matter what, if she accused him of taking drugs, she would probably undermine his already shaky self-confidence.

She did not want to mention her suspicions to his father, who had hired her, because she did not want to break the confidentiality of her relationship with Tim. Yet she was quite sure that if Tim went to an interview looking the way he had today, he would never be invited to a second interview, because an interviewer who observed the same characteristics Valerie had noted certainly would not think favorably of Tim. If Tim was going to undermine himself, she would not be able to fulfill her contract of helping him secure a suitable position—and that is what his father was paying her to do.

On the other hand, maybe Tim was just having a bad day. She knew him pretty well after six sessions, and usually he was more alert and responsive. When she asked if something was wrong, he said that everything was fine. Perhaps he was ill and did not want to admit it, but how would that explain the dilated pupils and slowed response she had observed on one other occasion? Uncertain about how to proceed, she kept trying to find excuses for his behavior.

Then the session ended, and she did not say anything further. She was feeling quite upset about the situation. Afterward she wrote down everything she believed was relevant to settling her dilemma:

- Tim was quite shy and had limited interpersonal skills.
- Tim's father wanted Tim to find a suitable job.
- Tim was taking action on most of her suggestions.

- The job she was being paid to do was to help Tim find a job.
- Tim had the technical skills to do the jobs he was applying for.
- Tim had come to two meetings with his pupils dilated.
- Tim's response to her had seemed slower during the meetings when his pupils were dilated.

Valerie then listed what she suspected but was not sure about:

- She suspected that Tim was using drugs.
- She suspected that another interviewer would have the same doubts that she did.
- She suspected that Tim would not get hired unless the problem she observed was dealt with.
- She suspected that telling Tim about her suspicions would do more harm than good.

Valerie was also aware that her personal and professional values demanded that she not pretend she was doing her job if she did not believe she could help achieve a successful outcome for Tim. At the same time she believed it was not ethical for her to do something that might cause harm to anyone else, and certainly not to a client. She decided that she could not ignore the situation, but that she could not discuss her suspicions without possibly harming her client.

In the end she decided to treat her observations like any other data she observed about her client. When she noticed him act in other inappropriate ways during practice interviews she did not hesitate to give him feedback about her observations. She had already told him that when he looked away from the interviewer while answering a question, the interviewer would probably think there was something wrong. She decided to treat her observations about his dilated pupils and lack of attentiveness the same way.

Early in their next session Valerie told Tim, "As your coach, I'm being paid only to tell you the truth. Whether or not you want to hear it, and whether or not you like me is not the issue. I would do you an injustice not to tell you the truth." Then Valerie told Tim that she had observed that his eyes had been dilated during the preceding meeting and at one other meeting as well. She also told him that during those meetings he seemed less sharp than usual. She said that she did not know what was causing the problem, but that it concerned her. She told Tim that an interviewer might feel uncomfortable about his appearance, and it might hurt his chances of being hired. She suggested that he see his physician or an eye specialist to find out if something could be done to correct the problem.

Nothing further was said, and at each additional session Tim appeared bright and alert. He eventually was hired for an appropriate job. Valerie was very relieved. Although she never learned the "truth," she suspected that Tim had taken the information she provided and used it to change his self-defeating behavior.

Compassionate Truth-Telling

Not every truth needs to be told. Considering your motivation for wanting to tell someone something and the potential for benefit or damage to the person who will hear it can help you decide whether or not to share a particular truth at a particular time. Once you decide to share the truth, your challenge is to find a way to share it that will allow both you and the recipient to maintain self-esteem and respect for each other.

Your own reason for telling the truth could be a contractual obligation, such as the situation Valerie experienced. It could also be based on your awareness that without your information someone will probably sustain harm or cause harm to another. For example, you might feel obligated to stop someone who is intoxicated from driving a car, even though that person may not want to know the truth about his or her condition. Sometimes you hope that telling the truth will influence someone to change his or her behavior, just so that it will be easier or more pleasant for you to relate to that person.

Think about how you can express your observations and concerns in a way that communicates your belief that the other person is valuable and important to you. First you have to believe it yourself. Even if you are angry at someone else's behavior or afraid of what he or she will do to you, it is important to view the other person as another human being who is doing the best he or she can under the circumstances.

This shift in perspective can help bring respect and aliveness to working relationships. You tend to withdraw from a relationship when you feel judged or criticized and move closer when you feel appreciated. Closer relationships make all mutual activities more rewarding. You can appreciate someone for who he or she is and simultaneously disagree with what that person does. Doing this takes a commitment to honoring the intrinsic worth of other people at all times.

Guidelines offered by Sid Simon, Ph.D. (1987), suggest that it is important to consider several questions before you tell a truth that someone else might find painful or difficult to hear:

1. *Is this information new to this person, or does he or she already know about it?* Sometimes people are very aware of an important truth. Take, for instance, someone who you believe needs to stop smoking. Telling someone something he or she already knows is not likely to produce a positive outcome. Perhaps it would be more useful to tell the person the truth about your own feelings and concerns about the troublesome behavior than to say, "You smoke too much." You could say, "I don't like the smell of stale cigarette smoke in my office, so please don't come in right after you have had a cigarette."

2. *Is the person in shape to listen to you?* When someone is exhausted, distracted, very emotional, or under the influence of chemicals, he or she will probably not respond favorably to anything you say. If you tell someone the truth without considering his or her ability to use the information you are imparting, the other person may feel as if you are using the truth as a weapon to damage him or her.

3. *Are you willing to stay with the conversation as long as it takes to bring it to a satisfactory conclusion?* It is easy, but not humane, to drop the truth on someone like a bomb and then leave him or her alone to face the consequences of your revelation. Sometimes it is very important to stay and clarify or explain your position. Compassionate, respectful truth-telling is more than a hit-and-run affair.

Telling the truth constructively, in a way that maintains the other person's self-esteem and respect, is important if you intend to maintain a relationship with the person. It helps to separate your observations (facts), your assumptions, your conclusions, and your feelings about the situation. Facts are the data that anyone watching a video recording of the situation could also observe. Assumptions are stories people tell themselves about the observable information. It may be much easier for someone to accept your observations about something uncomfortable than to hear either your assumptions or your conclusions based on those observations. Assumptions and conclusions often sound like accusations instead of truth.

Learning to distinguish between facts and assumptions, before you reach any conclusions, helps you decide how to proceed in uncomfortable situations. For example, you have probably had the experience of greeting someone you know, only to have him or her pass by without acknowledging you or your greeting. The story you tell yourself about this situation depends on a variety of things that can include your past experiences with this person, how you are feeling about yourself at the moment, and your beliefs about whether or not the universe is a friendly place. You might tell yourself "He is angry at me," "He did not see me," "He is concentrating on his thoughts," or maybe "I must have made a mistake. I guess I did not know the person." You will not really know which explanation is correct until you gather further information.

Concluding that one of your explanations (assumptions) is the truth and acting on the basis of that conclusion without adequate information can cause misunderstanding and embarrassment. Knowing that assumptions are not facts, you can ask further questions to clarify your understanding of the truth. Saying, "You have not attended the last two meetings" (observation), and then asking, "Do you intend to resign from this committee?" (questioning an assumption), it is easier for the other person to respond to you than if you had declared flatly, "I guess you don't care what happens to this project" (conclusion).

To solve her problem, Valerie used her ability to distinguish facts from assumptions. Valerie knew that her suspicion that Tim was using drugs was just a tentative conclusion—a theory, not a fact. Her theory was based on noticing Tim's behavior, and knowing how people on drugs behave. She knew her assumption was not a fact, so in gently confronting Tim, she was careful to refer only to facts that she had observed and not to state her conclusions. Although separating facts from assumptions is an important skill, Valerie credits her success in solving this dilemma to long practice and her commitment to truth-telling with compassion for herself and others. Working in large corporations, she was well aware that telling certain unpopular truths could result in losing a job or an opportunity for advancement. Yet she learned that she could not live comfortably with deception.

On the way to becoming a skilled truth teller, Valerie learned to think very carefully about the potential impact she could have on another person by imparting uncomfortable information. She was very concerned that Tim's already fragile self-esteem might be damaged if she was wrong about the drug abuse and pointed out a physical condition that really was out of his control. Instead of attributing the symptoms to some known cause, she merely stated what she had observed, suggested a course of action (have it checked by a physician), and allowed Tim to preserve his dignity.

Valerie had also learned to consider the possible negative impact that telling any particular truth might have on herself. Before telling the truth, she decided whether or not she could live with the potential risks. She usually could. In this case she knew that if she told him about her observations, Tim might decide to end his sessions with her. Although she considered the financial impact of losing a client, that was not her main concern. Losing her integrity by giving a client less than her best would be a much more serious problem.

Valerie reports that the more she practices truth-telling, the easier and less scary it gets. She firmly believes: "If I take care of my clients and tell the truth with compassion, then business will follow, and repeat business will follow, too."

Learning to Recognize Your Assumptions and Tell the Truth with Compassion

1. When you have an immediate, strong response to something you encounter, ask yourself why you feel the way you do.

Then ask yourself what the event meant to you—what story did you tell yourself about it?

2. Listen to the words you use to tell yourself and others why something has occurred. Whenever you hear a conclusion such as "that means . . . ," think about how you know what you think you know about the situation. Ask yourself what conclusions you think other people would reach if they examined the same information.

3. Check on the accuracy of your conclusions before you take any action.

4. Decide what you want to accomplish by telling the truth. Valerie was very clear about her goal. She wanted Tim to look and sound appropriate at job interviews.

5. Think about how you can express your observations and concerns in a way that communicates your belief that the other person is valuable and important to you.

6. Think about the probable effect that hearing this truth will have on your listener.

7. Think about the possible consequences you will experience as a result of telling the truth. If you believe that you need to tell the truth even though you risk bringing on negative consequences, have a plan in mind to cope with them.

8. Treat yourself with respect and compassion. Developing this skill takes time, practice, and courage. Allow yourself to practice without self-criticism.

9. Once you make your decision and figure out what you need to do, go ahead and implement it. Tell the truth—with compassion.

Reference

Simon, S. "Forgiveness." Workshop presented at the National Conference on Addictions, Colorado Springs, Colo., August 25, 1987.

CHAPTER

18

All I Did Was . . . Why Did She React That Way?

Judith did not suspect that Marian, her new assistant adminis-trator, was living in the past. Judith knew that Marian re-sponded very poorly to suggestions. Marian was sure that Judith did not like her, and she was ready to resign. Only some careful consultation helped them uncover Marian's truth—that she had Judith confused with her own grandmother.

Judith, the director of a nursing home, was in a quandary. She knew that she needed to suggest some changes to her assistant director, Marian, but she was afraid that doing so would cause further deterioration in their relationship. In the five months since Marian had been hired, the two women had never developed a comfortable rapport with each other. Each time they spoke they seemed to grow more distant, and Judith could almost see Marian oozing resentment at her.

Judith hoped that she would not have to fire her assistant. Marian had been hired after a long search, she came with excellent recommendations, and she was doing well in most areas. She seemed to be well liked by the staff members she supervised. If she did not have so much difficulty accepting Judith's suggestions, Marian would still be a good choice for the position.

Judith wondered if she had done something to contribute to the difficulty with Marian, so she decided to try once more to find out what was wrong. In a private meeting, Judith asked Marian if she would talk about how they were working together. Marian's response startled Judith: "I know you don't like me. You are always displeased with my work. I will resign today if you like."

Judith tried to explain that she did not want Marian's resignation, and that Marian's work was generally satisfactory, but she knew that Marian would not really believe her. Judith was bewildered. She could not understand why Marian thought that she disliked either her or her work. Judith usually had extremely good relationships with her staff members, and she could not remember ever having been in a similar situation.

When Judith explained the problem to me, I suspected that both women were having difficulty reading and responding to each other's subtle emotional signals. In a meeting arranged to help Judith develop an appropriate style of managing Marian, I observed that Marian shifted frequently in her chair and rarely looked directly at her supervisor. Judith said to Marian, "I don't understand why you think I'm unhappy with your job performance." As she spoke, she leaned forward, and Marian shifted backward. When I asked Marian why she pulled away, she replied, "I guess it's because I felt like I was being criticized."

Marian was misreading Judith's body language signals of interest and was responding to them as if she were being criticized. As both women began to pay close attention to what was happening in addition to the words they were speaking to each other, Marian began to smile. She confided to Judith, "I did not realize how much you remind me of my grandmother. No matter what I did, I could not please her. She usually looked really intently at me when she criticized me." Marian looked at Judith again, this time seeing Judith in a new way, and asked, "Are you really just interested in me?" Judith affirmed that she really was interested, and that she wanted to develop a good working relationship. After additional discussions about how to correctly interpret each other's nonverbal cues, Marian asked Judith to give her lots of regular verbal feedback about what she was doing well. Judith had no problem with this, since it was her usual management style. She felt hopeful that Marian would be able to accept her positive acknowledgment as well as feedback about problems without confusing the current situation with a negative experience from her past.

It took Marian quite a while to stop emotionally confusing Judith with her grandmother, but because she understood the problem, Marian was able to begin to control her inappropriate reactions. Over the next few weeks the two managed to develop an effective working relationship.

Projection

Sometimes you can do everything right and things go wrong anyway. Judith could not figure out what she was doing wrong in this situation, because she was not doing anything inappropriate. She was simply being herself, and because she reminded Marian of someone in the past, Marian was having a problem with her. Unfortunately, this happens quite frequently, and it is not anyone's fault. Our brains trick us. We are biologically programmed to react before we think about what we are reacting to.

We learn to recognize patterns when we are very young. We use this skill to distinguish one person from another, to tell the difference between safe and dangerous situations, and to react to protect ourselves when we are in danger. This ability has helped the human species survive and thrive as we evolved. Although in many situations this warning system is still useful, when the similarity to a past incident is coincidental and no real danger exists, an automatic response can cause an immense amount of confusion.

Marian's perception about her relationship with Judith was based on a truth that had existed in the past, not in the present. Whenever she looked at Judith she was not really seeing Judith at all, and she truthfully did not know that she was falling into this

144   Tools for Becoming a Truth Teller

trap. Instead of reacting to Judith, she was reacting to an old
pattern she had learned to recognize when she was a child. Based
on good evidence, Marian knew that no matter what she did, she
could not please her grandmother. This set up an emotional pattern for responding to "Grandmother": whenever she had seen
Grandmother's face in the past she felt both scared and resentful.
Now when she looked at Judith she "saw" Grandmother instead
and felt the anger and resentment from the past.

Psychologists use the term *projection* to describe the process of
unconsciously reacting to someone as if he or she is someone else.
It is almost as if the face of the person in front of you is a blank screen
and you project a picture from your past experience onto the screen.
You then react to your projection instead of really seeing the person
you are with. You truly believe that your reactions are about the
person in front of you. Meanwhile, the person in front of you
experiences your reaction and usually has his or her own reaction
to your behavior. Confusion and misunderstanding proliferate.

This situation is very common whenever one person supervises
another in the workplace. It is especially easy for us to accidentally
project our own parents' faces onto the faces of our supervisors.
Just being in a situation where we must do what another person
wants us to do unconsciously reminds us of being children who
have to obey our elders. Most of us harbor some unresolved and
largely forgotten fears and resentments from childhood experiences. When those fears or resentments are reactivated by things
supervisors do and say in the course of their ordinary job responsibilities, weird things may happen.

These strange experiences happen to everyone occasionally, and
to some people frequently. Supervisors are not exempt. Anyone
may remind anyone else of someone who caused problems in the
past. Perhaps a sibling or schoolmate bullied you, and a coworker
has characteristics that are similar to that long-ago nemesis. You
may dislike your coworker for no apparent reason. You may even
feel like responding to a small action your coworker initiates as if
it were cause for a major emergency. If you are coping with other
stress or are feeling particularly tired or vulnerable, you may lose
control and dump those inappropriate emotions from the past into
the present situation. It is just as likely that you will randomly
become the victim of someone else's projection. If someone seems

to be angry at you, or afraid of you, and you do not have any idea why, projection might be the cause. Of course, there is also the possibility that you have actually done something inappropriate, and you are not aware of it.

Sorting out who is projecting what past experience onto whom may take more time and energy than it is worth. In many cases people who dislike each other simply avoid working closely together. If you feel that you are treated inappropriately once in a while, chalk it up to the other person's stress level. Then ignore it. If the problem recurs frequently with someone you need to work with on a regular basis, then figuring out what to do about it makes sense.

Addressing the Problem When You Seem to Be Wearing Someone Else's Face

If you believe that someone may be treating you as if you are someone else, try taking these actions to ease the situation. CAUTION: If either of you is too upset to have a rational conversation, wait until you are both calm. Find a way to put some distance between you—even if it means taking a break and going to the bathroom.

1. Treat the person seriously. Respond to his or her criticism or attack by asking for clarification of the problem he or she is experiencing. You may want to review the suggestions for asking questions at the end of Chapter 16.

2. Do your best not to respond defensively. Pretend you are a detective and focus on gathering information. Save your emotional response for another time and place.

3. If someone points to behavior that you consider appropriate, but he or she considers it inappropriate, apologize anyway. You can still be truthful if you apologize for unintentionally causing him or her distress. After all, you probably do not intend to do things that upset others.

4. If you believe you need to continue the behavior that the other person considers offensive, discuss what you are

attempting to accomplish with that behavior, and ask for the person's help in achieving your goal in some other way.

5. In the future, remember that this person has a sore spot or "button" in this area, and try to treat him or her carefully. You probably have buttons too and would prefer that others avoid pushing them.

6. If you cannot resolve the problem this way, consider asking a trusted third party to act as an arbitrator to help you both decide what to do next.

Addressing the Problem When You Are Doing the Projecting

If you suspect that you are projecting someone from your past onto the person you are actually sitting face-to-face with today, there are many things you can do to change the situation. When you feel an overwhelming flood of emotion in response to some other individual's ordinary behavior, you are probably responding to the present as if it were the past. Here are some clues you can look for to diagnose this problem:

*   Hating someone for no particular reason,

*   Crying or feeling like crying when someone ignores you,

*   Getting very angry over small annoyances,

*   Feeling overwhelmed by fear around certain types of people, and

*   Defending yourself when someone discovers you have made a mistake.

You may experience getting into these situations so quickly that it seems as if a rubber band has snapped you from the present into the past. Although you cannot stop this experience when it is happening, you can learn to recognize it and glean information from the incident instead of reacting as if you were in an emergency. After all, your response is just your nervous system getting you into trouble by trying to keep you out of trouble.

The following steps can help you move back into the present and detach the rubber band so that your future reactions will feel less intense.

1. Learn to recognize the out-of-proportion reaction or feeling when it happens.

2. Pause! This is a good time to count to ten. By the time you have finished counting you will be able to think again.

3. Remind yourself that your body (actually a primitive part of your brain) is trying to take care of you, and the danger is probably from the past. Just because your freeze, fight, or flight trigger has been pushed, you do not have to act on it. If you want more information about this, read the first chapter of *Emotional Intelligence* by Daniel Goleman (1995). Pausing may be all it takes to bring you back to the present. Then you can respond to the situation in whatever way you choose.

4. If you need more time to think clearly, make an excuse and take a break until you have calmed yourself.

5. If this situation happens frequently and you would like to detach the unknown connection between your past and your present, think about other times when you have experienced a similar flood of feelings. This process can take some time, so wait until you can arrange to be uninterrupted for at least an hour.

6. Let your memory take you back as far as it can. It may be helpful to go back to the earliest time you can remember experiencing those feelings. You may go back to high school, grade school, or even earlier.

7. When you find an early memory, re-create it in as much detail as you can. Notice who you are with, where you are, and how old you are. Notice what is happening that results in your feeling so emotional.

8. Think about what kind of comfort or support you needed at that earlier stressful time in your life, and imagine that you are receiving that support. You may feel emotional as you do this. That is normal.

9. Allow yourself to take as much time as you need to complete this process. You will know you are done when you feel a sense of completion or relief. The next time you encounter a similar situation you will not react so intensely.

10. Repeat this process as often as you like. If you continue to have difficulty, a competent therapist can help you complete the process of detaching the past from the present. Ask someone you trust for a referral.

Remember that if you are projecting, you are experiencing a normal part of being human. Learn to cope with it, and you will find it easier to accept yourself, your colleagues, and your family.

Reference

Goleman, D. *Emotional Intelligence*. New York: Bantam Books, 1995.

CHAPTER

19

Reality Isn't What It Used To Be, and Perhaps It Never Was

Frank, a key employee of a growing electrical contracting company, did not want to believe that times had changed. Although the owner's son, Sam, was getting ready to assume the company presidency, Frank insisted on treating him as if he were still a teenager just learning the business. Sam valued Frank's skill and experience, but he also needed Frank to accept his authority.

Frank Blanchard remembered the day he decided to leave Sam Harrison, a young apprentice, at the work site to finish his assigned job while Frank and the rest of the crew went to lunch. The other electricians told Frank only half-jokingly that he should look for another job. They warned him, "You just can't do that to the boss's son!" Frank did not feel that he was taking any risk. After six years of working with Pride Electric Company's owner, Peggy Harrison, he trusted her fairness and integrity. He was determined not to treat Sam any differently from the way he treated the other apprentices. He expected all of them to be responsible for doing their work in a timely way, and he provided similar consequences if they did not. Frank was right. Neither Sam nor Peggy said anything about the incident, but the story was retold for years in the company whenever anyone questioned Frank's fairness or authority.

There was never any question that Sam was being trained to take over the company in the future. After he graduated from college at twenty-one with "book smarts," Peggy, his mother, suggested that he learn "field smarts" by joining the apprentice program. He worked in the field for six years before becoming vice president of the company. His relationship with Frank did not change much for the next two years, as he learned the intricacies of estimating, selling, recruiting, and managing the business. But when Sam decided, with Peggy's cautious support, that he wanted to grow the company, he and Frank began to clash regularly.

Frank, a journeyman electrician, knew how to manage the technical operations of a small company. He could easily control the deployment of a dozen electricians and the equipment necessary to handle the workflow. He knew how to manage his crews, teach his apprentices, and estimate complex jobs. He liked knowing everything that was going on in the company and having input into all decisions.

As Sam started to assume more responsibility in the company, Frank resisted. Sam complained, "Frank wants to tell me what to do, but not why to do it. He tells me that I should not need to know the technical stuff, that I'm going to be running the company and I should leave the rest to him. In order to do my job, I think I should know what the guys in the field are thinking, know the technical end, and be sure that the customers are happy."

Sometimes Sam would take the easy way out, making decisions based on "who would give me the least flak," instead of thinking through what was best for the company. Sometimes Sam would tell Frank what to do. When Frank disagreed, usually because he did not think new procedures should apply to him, he would conveniently misinterpret or ignore Sam's instructions and do what he thought was best instead. Frank, very confident of his ability to solve problems and make technical decisions, was certain that he was doing what was best for the company. Sam struggled to make Frank understand that the expanding company needed to change some old procedures to meet the changing demands of the industry.

Finally the company suffered a serious cash flow crunch because Sam was trying to expand business too rapidly, and Sam faced a personal crisis as well. Sam finally admitted that he did not have the knowledge and experience necessary to transform the company into his vision of what the company should be. With Peggy's support, he began to attend conventions to learn as much as possible about the newest developments in the industry. He invited consultants to guide him in restructuring the company. He used their support to clarify his goals and to improve his ability to communicate the need for change to others in his company. He even learned to stay alert to the fuzzy, incomplete communications with Frank and to clarify the details before problems developed.

Things have changed in the past several years. Now a mature thirty-five-year-old vice president, Sam reports that he is receiving much less criticism from his employees. When he recently wanted to institute a new system for tracking tools within the company, Frank, who now manages company operations, objected. But Sam no longer suggests changes until he can demonstrate the need for them to the people involved. When he showed Frank that the company had spent $13,000 on tool replacement in the past year, Frank agreed to try the new system. When the rapid retrieval of just one tool saved enough money to pay for the new system, Frank was convinced of the value of the new system.

Sam feels that he has recently made a series of good decisions for the company because of his increased ability to understand how current changes will affect the future development of his organization. He knows that he needs to rely more and more on the information provided by the new systems he has put into place. He says, "As we grow, gut feelings won't always be valid—there are too many variables." Sam now carefully coaches everyone about how to provide information that is accurate and useful for guiding the company.

Frank would still prefer to rely on gut feelings, and initially he opposes many of Sam's decisions. Other senior members of the management team are Frank's contemporaries in age and experience. When they understand and support Sam's ideas, Frank becomes more receptive to changes. When he thoroughly understands the necessity for a new system, Frank cooperates as fully as he can, even though he privately wishes for a simpler and less regulated environment. Sam continues to rely on Frank's integrity and experience to manage the operations of the company, and Frank does not disappoint him.

Coping with Changing Realities

It has been said that one form of insanity is to do what you have always done and expect different results. In today's rapidly changing business environment, it can also be considered a form of insanity to do what you have always done and expect the same results. As thousands of people who have lost jobs through corporate restructuring (downsizing, rightsizing, whatever you want to call it) can attest, doing what they had always done did not help them keep their jobs. Likewise, businesses that have served a particular market for many years find that sudden shifts in purchasing patterns or the introduction of new products by competitors leave them scrambling to survive.

No matter how much we protest, change happens; and it happens faster now than ever before in history. Your past life experiences have an impact on how quickly you notice changes and how comfortably you respond to them. The way your family responded to changes when you were a child influences the way you respond to changes now, as does your experience and training throughout your career. Random and unpredictable life events also have an impact. Surviving a sudden and fundamental shift in your life circumstances may give you confidence in your ability to cope with whatever comes along. If you have successfully reconstructed your life after a job loss or serious accident, other changes may seem much easier to manage.

If you are accustomed to being in situations where people ignore change and don't even notice that it is occurring, you may have difficulty even recognizing change when it is happening. It is hard to be comfortable with change if you grew up in a family where tradition was honored and change was treated as a threat and harshly criticized. In that kind of environment, you learn that reality is fixed and unchanging and that there is only one right way to see things. You learn to perceive change as a threat and to value permanency and the status quo.

Often it is easier to turn your attention to something else at the first hint of a threat, so that you can continue to feel safe. As long as you can manage to keep your attention on the reality that used to be, you feel comfortable. When you are forced to respond to a new reality because your job skills become obsolete or your company goes out of business, you feel frightened and angry and may not know what to do next. The first thing you think of is probably how to change things back to the way they used to be. Responding this way is normal, but this kind of behavior may be perceived as strange by someone who has learned to accept change as fun and exciting.

Frank lives in a world where he has learned what is right and wrong and considers it important to transmit this information to others. As long as that is his job, he functions very well. It is very important for him to know that he is right. It is difficult for him to try new ways of doing things, because of the implication that if the new way is right, the old way must be wrong.

On the other hand, growing up in a family that discussed changes as they occurred makes it easier for you to notice changes yourself. If changes were noticed but greeted with fear and lamentation, you may find yourself reacting the same way. If changes were seen as opportunities for pleasure or improvement, then you probably do not feel particularly threatened by shifting realities. You may even enjoy the challenge of learning to ride the waves of change to create a reality that works for you.

If you learned that there are many possible ways of interpreting challenges to the status quo, then you may be open to considering a variety of different responses to a situation that others may find fearful or threatening. You may also feel bewildered, angry, or impatient that others cannot understand the possibilities that you can so easily appreciate.

Sam's mother, Peggy, is an entrepreneur. She modeled flexible responses to changing circumstances as she grew her business and raised her family. Recognizing and dealing with change is second nature to her son, Sam. When he was younger, though, he thought that everyone enjoyed change as much as he did.

If your life experience includes situations where change was anticipated or created, then you may be a change agent yourself. When you are comfortable with change and even seek to impose it on others in order to create your own vision, you may be shocked by the resistance you encounter from people who would prefer to keep things the way they are. When you understand why some people have a more difficult time accepting change than others do, it is easier to understand why the way you present a change influences whether or not it will be accepted.

Sam has learned that in order to get support for an innovation from his management team, including Frank, he needs to think it through in detail and present it clearly. He describes the present situation and then outlines the results he anticipates from making the change. Then he asks others to critique his thinking. He asks if his goal sounds appropriate and attainable, and if they can think of any problems he has not anticipated. He uses the feedback he receives, since he has learned that criticism of his ideas is not a personal attack. More and more of his ideas are being accepted and supported within the company.

Influencing Your Own Reality

Have you ever noticed that when you get a new car you suddenly notice cars just like yours everywhere? The world probably does not have any more cars like yours than it had the day before you started noticing the other ones. The reality of the world did not change, but your perception of reality did.

You actually organize your own reality from one moment to the next. You do it each time you choose what to notice about your environment based on what is currently important to you. When you are hungry, your reality consists of restaurants, food stores, and when you will eat next. If you work in sales, you are probably constantly scanning materials you read and people you meet for information that will help you make more sales and increase your commissions. If you are planning a large meeting, you probably have conference facilities that may be suitable for your use running around in your head. Under other circumstances, you might be completely oblivious to information about food, sales, or conference facilities.

You never know all there is to know about the world around you. Your nervous system is designed to screen out extra information to keep you from being overwhelmed with more stimulation than you can organize. Imagine two different people reading the same newspaper. Neither notices everything in the paper. One person may read the front page, the sports section, and the comics. The other may read the local news, the entertainment section, and the obituaries. Neither reads everything, but each believes that he or she has read the newspaper.

No matter what you believe is real and important, someone else can be standing right next to you and decide that different information is significant. You can be unaware that the person next to you may see things very differently from the way you do. If you know that the difference exists, you can then either accept it, choose to argue about what you believe is really important, or be curious about what the other person considers significant, and why. The more you learn about other people's views of reality, the broader your own view becomes.

Some people consider other people's views a joy and a blessing. Others consider this information to be a threat. It depends on what you have learned to consider important. People who are not threatened by multiple views of reality are horrified that wars are fought to preserve a particular viewpoint. People who fight wars to uphold a particular point of view cannot understand why others do not understand the threat they perceive.

What to Do When Your Reality Changes

1. Acknowledge what has changed. If your circumstances change suddenly, your immediate reaction may be "Oh no, that can't be so." (The company can't be going bankrupt! My boss can't be leaving!) The sooner you can move past the normal reaction of denial, the faster you will be able to adapt to the world as it really is now.

2. Find a safe way to express your emotions about the change. When emotions are suppressed, they may cause stress-related damage to your body, like headaches or stomachaches, or turn into depression. When you let yourself feel anger, fear, and sadness, these feelings tend to dissipate.

3. Find a way to adjust to your new reality, even if you do not want to. You might ask questions about how the change will affect you instead of trying to ignore it. By collecting more information, you will feel less helpless and will be in a better position to take steps to protect your own interests.

4. Dare to dream. Think of the new reality you want to create for yourself. Use whatever tools you need to do this. Authors Barbara Sher (1979, 1994) and Marsha Sinetar (1995) offer many useful techniques for discovering a vision that is right for you.

5. Shift your focus so you notice those aspects of the world that support your new vision. When you find yourself discouraged, gently remind yourself that you can create something that will work for you, even if it takes longer than you would like.

6. Find someone to support you in making the changes you want to make. Someone else who is trying to implement personal change is often a good source of support. Make an agreement to support each other. A chosen mentor or professional coach can also help you stay focused and take the steps you need to take.

7. Just do it! Even the best planning must eventually evolve into action if you mean to take charge of changing your own experience of reality.

References

Sher, B. *Wishcraft.* New York: Viking Press, 1979.

——*I Could Do Anything If I Only Knew What It Was.* New York: Delacorte Press, 1994.

Sinetar, M. *To Build the Life You Want, Create the Work You Love.* New York: St. Martin's Press, 1995.

CHAPTER

20

The "What I Feel Like Saying" Process

Staff meetings were becoming a waste of time in Monica's mortgage banking office. Staff members would come late, leave early, and barely pretend to participate. Introducing a simple exercise at the start of each weekly meeting allowed everyone to gradually learn to work together more effectively.

Monica dreaded going into the office, especially for the required weekly staff meetings. As a loan officer in a mortgage banking firm, she was grateful that she could spend most of her time calling on clients. She felt increasingly frustrated by the lack of support she was experiencing in the office. The loan processors seemed to be forgetting more and more details, and she and the other loan officers were being required to spend their time putting out fires so the loans could actually close. Meetings were becoming gripe sessions dragging down everyone's morale.

With almost five years of experience, Monica was the second most experienced broker in the office. When she dutifully arrived at a weekly meeting almost exactly on time, only three of the other eleven staff members were present: Lois, the operations manager; Michelle, one of the processors; and Eileen, the receptionist. A few minutes later Jim and Mike, two other loan officers, arrived. A half hour after the meeting was supposed to have begun, everyone was finally in the room, but Jack, the production manager, was sitting there talking on his portable phone. Monica was furious. What a waste of time! As the routine business of the meeting finally got under way and was droning on, people started getting up for coffee, having whispered side conversations, and answering pages. Monica finally decided she'd had enough. She said loudly, "This is NOT WORKING!" Everyone looked at her shocked, and then they started agreeing with what she had said. She and Mike said almost simultaneously to Jack, "We need a consultant to get us back on track."

Jack pointed out that the consultant solution had not worked in the past. "All he did was moderate the gripe session, and nothing changed." Elaine, another broker, agreed, but she said she thought she had a friend who could help find a more suitable consultant. Jack, more than a little irritated, finally agreed that if a decent consultant could be found, he would cooperate, but he did not want to waste his time on the matter.

One phone call led to another, and finally Monica called me and asked if I could help them learn to cooperate with each other. She explained the situation to me. There were five loan officers or brokers (three men and two women) who located people who needed mortgage loans and connected them with lenders who had funds. Four loan processors (all women) did the complex paperwork that was necessary to secure the loans. Two closers (also women) did the final specialized work required so that all parties could sign the papers and complete the mortgage process.

Jack, the production manager of the office, was a loan officer with fifteen years of experience. Lois, the operations manager, was a former loan processor with ten years in the business; she kept the business aspects of the office running smoothly. Everyone else had three to five years of experience except Eileen, the receptionist, who had been with the firm for just one year.

Monica explained that the atmosphere in the office had been steadily deteriorating over the past two years. The salaried support people were jealous of the brokers because they earned more by working on commission. The brokers were angry because the support people were pushing them to do things that they believed the support staff should be doing. The loan processors and closers also blamed each other for problems with incomplete paperwork. As I listened to Monica, I automatically paraphrased the ending of an old song into "and no one likes anybody very much." I asked her about that, and she explained that no one person in the office was really a problem. Most of the staff members were really quite pleasant away from the office, but in the office there was so much anger and tension that they could not seem to get past it. She then told me that the group wanted me to come to one of their weekly two-hour meetings and demonstrate that I could be of help to them. I decided to accept the challenge, and a week later I attended their meeting.

After introductions I requested that they divide into four small groups and identify the three issues they thought were causing the problems in the office. This information was written down on large sheets of paper and taped to the walls. Each list started with "communication"; other items included "scheduling," "unfriend-liness," "lateness," and "anger." I wanted them to understand that they could identify their own problems. My job was to facilitate their communication so that they could reach their own solutions.

Creating Safety Encourages Truth-Telling

We started by using a simple sharing exercise that helps people clear their minds of other issues so they can focus on the meeting instead of being distracted. The process is modeled after one used by the phenomenally successful recovery groups of Alcoholics Anonymous. It is also similar to a Native American custom of using a "talking stick." Whoever holds the stick has the right to speak without interruption until he or she is finished. We went around the table, in order, and each person had the opportunity to share whatever he or she felt like saying. Not everyone chose to speak.

The first comments were cautious. "I was surprised that all the groups said similar things." "I was worried about everyone getting into arguments, and I'm glad it is not happening." "This meeting feels as if we might get somewhere." "I thought I was the only one who felt that way. I'm glad I'm not alone." As each person spoke, the tension eased just a tiny bit. When the last person had spoken, I joined this process as a member as well as a facilitator. "What I feel like saying is that I'm glad that everyone seems to be feeling more comfortable with our meeting. Let's continue this process for a while longer."

On the next time around the table, Monica took the risk of talking about her own feelings. "I have been so frustrated and angry that I have considered resigning. The main reason that I stay is that the money is so good. I wish it felt better to come to the office." After three other people had the floor it was Jim's turn. "I would not blame Monica for leaving. I think people here are really unfriendly."

Several people started to speak at once, and I reminded them of the agreement to take turns. Eileen, the receptionist, was next and spoke timidly: "I try to say hello to every one of you as you come in, but half of you walk right by and never even nod."

When it was my turn again, I acknowledged Monica, Jim, and Eileen for talking about uncomfortable issues. Then I wondered aloud if others were experiencing similar problems and suggested that we continue to use the same process of taking turns to explore the situation. When it was his turn, Jack, the skeptical production manager, imitated what I had done, and also thanked Monica for speaking about her frustration. Then he turned to Eileen and said that he knew he was one of the guilty ones who sometimes ignored her. He promised to return her greetings in the future.

Others responded to Jack's promise by acknowledging him and making pledges of their own to at least respond to Eileen's greetings. When my turn came around again, I called attention to the time and suggested that we go around once more. On that circuit almost everyone said something about how promising the session had seemed, and expressed a wish to continue addressing the office problems in this way. I stopped the process and negotiated an agreement to return to their meeting in a month.

A month later, people were chatting with each other when I arrived. I suggested using the "What I Feel Like Saying" process again to get started. This time people started talking about their frustrations about trying to get to an early-morning meeting. Ordinary stuff about a spouse being out of town and needing to take extra responsibility for the children, about heavy traffic and a near accident, and about looking forward to an impending vacation emerged during the first sharing as we went around the table. Something else emerged, too. People expressed empathy with each other's feelings, and they talked about their own similar challenges. When it was my turn, I talked about the friendlier and more empathetic comments I was hearing, and I wondered aloud about whether anything else in the office had changed.

In the next two rounds several people commented about how much more pleasant the general atmosphere at the office seemed to be. Then Jim shifted the discussion to a new level. "It is nicer, but I still had to go back to two clients this week to clean up mistakes caused by a loan processor. That part hasn't changed." When it was Monica's turn, she started to describe why she thought those problems still existed. Lois acknowledged her frustration about managing the shifting workflow and said that she had some ideas about how things could be improved.

As facilitator, I suggested that we end the "What I Feel Like Saying" process we were using and shift to an ordinary problem-solving discussion. They were amazed at how quickly they heard and accepted Lois's suggestions. Several of the loan processors contributed their ideas as well, and everyone agreed to experiment with these new ways to implement the workflow. Again, I agreed to return in a month.

My monthly meetings with the group continued for a year. They would meet three times per month without me, and then we would meet together. The pattern of the meetings continued to be similar to our second session. First people would bring each other up to date on personal issues. Some of these were quite sensitive, including the need to place Elaine's aging grandmother in a nursing home, Jack's dismay about his son's alcohol abuse, and the breakdown of Mike's marriage. They also shared Eileen's joy at her engagement. After a few rounds on personal issues they would start discussing problems that were still occurring in the office.

When the "problem of the day" emerged, we would switch to discussing ways of solving the problem.

Sometimes I made suggestions. I offered the group members copies of the agreements used to facilitate communication in another organization, and they adopted some of them. (A detailed description of these agreements appears in Chapter 22.) Usually they quickly solved their own problems.

At the end of the year, I was quite confident that they could solve their own problems, but they weren't sure. I felt like I was being treated like a security blanket, but by that time I enjoyed them so much that I didn't mind. We met every other month for a while, and then quarterly. Finally we agreed to end our meetings, and when I checked with them two years later, they were still doing just fine.

Transforming Meetings by Encouraging Truth-Telling

When communication in the office broke down originally, no one felt either safe enough or powerful enough to change the dysfunctional patterns. Those patterns of jealously about money, competitiveness, and lack of trust fed on themselves, even though no one was really trying to hurt anyone else. Most people were feeling hurt, angry, or mistreated, and their interest and energy lagged as a result. But it wasn't really necessary to discuss the reasons for or the details of the communication breakdown in order to address the issues.

What people needed was a way to feel safe enough to talk to each other. Once that safety was established, both through my presence and by establishing a safe structure—the "What I Feel Like Saying" process—they were able to see each other as real people instead of as enemies. Their inherent intelligence and compassion emerged and blossomed in the newly established safe space, and they were able to tell the truth and solve problems together quite naturally.

You can use this extremely simple process in a variety of ways to create a safe enough structure for any group to begin to solve problems together. You do not need to be the facilitator or the group leader to get started. All you need to do is to suggest using this process as an experiment. It is useful for you to know why you want to introduce the process, but try not to expect a specific result. Although you can deliberately influence the process using the following suggestions, when you allow the process to develop on its own, surprises sometimes occur.

Use the "What I Feel Like Saying" process to help all members of a group free themselves from outside distractions at the start of a meeting. If that is your purpose, introduce the program as an experiment to make the meeting more efficient, and follow the instructions but limit the time to just five or ten minutes. If you set a timer to signal the end of the process, it will allow everyone present to share responsibility for stopping the process. Most people get very interested and do not want to stop.

You can use the "What I Feel Like Saying" process to increase the cohesiveness of a group. Introduce it as a way to get to know each other better, and continue with it until the process comes to a natural close with every participant saying, "I pass," for a full round. If you want to speed the process, take cautious risks yourself. The more any person shares sensitive information, the more likely others will be moved to do the same. It is natural to use each other as models and play follow the leader in this process. Anyone can spontaneously move into a leadership position.

You can also use the process as a way to help a group talk about difficult issues safely. To do this, you must carefully keep track of what each person contributes. If the group consists of more than six people, it is useful to keep notes. When it is your turn to speak, acknowledge the comments that are moving in the direction of addressing the difficult issues. It is also useful to summarize the discussion before making your own contributions.

If you want to encourage a more intensive discussion, acknowledge the people who take risks. Model risk-taking yourself after others have done so. Waiting for others to go first helps you keep your enthusiasm in check. It is important to allow the process to move slowly at first. Others will soon imitate you and begin summarizing their observations and acknowledging each other. As more and more people take responsibility in the situation, the process speeds up naturally. You can start to bring the process to a close by suggesting ending when it is your turn. Others can agree or make alternate proposals when it is their turn to speak.

Using the "What I Feel Like Saying" process in any group is likely to make it easier for the group to do its work effectively. This is not a process for solving problems. It is a process that encourages a deeper group understanding of both people and situations, and is a very useful prelude to addressing any decisions a group needs to make. When you need to solve problems or reach decisions, end the "What I Feel Like Saying" process first, and then address those issues in an ordinary way.

Using the "What I Feel Like Saying" Process in Your Own Group

1. Explain why you want to introduce the process.

2. Ask permission to use it as an experiment for a certain length of time.

3. Make sure that everyone understands this process.

    a. Each person present will share anything that they currently feel like saying with others in the group.

    b. Others will listen respectfully to whatever is said.

    c. There will be no interruptions except to ask for brief clarifications if necessary.

    d. Go around the room in an orderly fashion, giving each person a turn to speak.

    e. Anyone who does not want to speak may simply say, "I pass."

    f. The process ends when each person in the group says, "I pass." Some groups set a time limit; when the time is up the process stops. Sometimes a designated facilitator or leader suggests when to stop the process.

4. If people start to interrupt each other, call attention to the problem and suggest returning to the process.

5. Evaluate how the process worked and whether you wish to use it again.

CHAPTER

21

Is Something Sinister Going On?

Everyone at the meeting was frustrated. People were repeating their points several times, but they were not reaching any resolution. A simple matter that should have taken five minutes had been debated for an hour. After a brief recess, Barry raised a new issue that concerned everyone. When the discussion of the new topic was completed, they went back to considering the original issue, and they reached agreement on a solution almost immediately.

Barry sat in the meeting on a new incentive program wondering how to escape. Things had been going downhill for at least thirty minutes, and now Agnes, his boss, was raising the same issue again. The same points were being reiterated for at least the third time. Barry was getting furious and mentally blaming all eight people in the room for their stupidity. He had already explained his position to the group several times, each time with increasing intensity. This really was a simple matter. Why were they taking such an interminably long time to come to a decision? He looked around the table and saw that almost everyone was fidgeting and appeared to be unhappy.

He tried to calm down enough to think of a way to explain things differently, hoping he could find a way to make everyone understand that arguing was pointless. Then Barry remembered an agreement he had made with himself: "When I notice I am becoming angry, I will switch from explaining to questioning." He supposed that it was time to put his new policy into action. Unfortunately, he was so frustrated that he couldn't think of a question that seemed useful. He decided that he needed a chance to get away from the situation.

Finally Barry interrupted the discussion and requested a short break. Agnes looked annoyed, but she agreed, and everyone else headed out of the room with apparent relief. As they walked down the hall, Barry asked Jim if he had any clue about why they were so stuck. Jim wasn't sure what was wrong with the meeting. He commented that he personally was more worried about the potential budget shortfall and possible layoffs than about whether or not the company should offer a new incentive system. Barry was worried about potential layoffs, too. Perhaps everyone was focusing on the incentive system because it was easier than talking about the bad news. He resolved that once the meeting was reconvened, he would talk over his concern with the group before they returned to their earlier discussion.

As everyone settled back into the meeting, Barry said, "Before we go on, I want to mention what I was thinking about during the break. I realized that I am really concerned about the possible upcoming layoffs. I wonder if anyone else is worried too." When Agnes looked around the table and saw everyone nodding, she decided to let this discussion continue. Jim spoke first, followed in rapid succession by four others. All acknowledged their concerns. Agnes agreed that they had reason to be concerned, but she pointed out that the situation was still uncertain. She promised to let them all know as soon as she received any definite information. When the discussion returned to the incentive system, it took the group only five minutes to reach agreement.

Barry left the meeting thinking about how telling the truth about his own concerns had created an opportunity for others to do likewise. He wondered if there was a connection between discussing unspoken worries and the quick solution to the main issue of the meeting. He decided to look for his own hidden concerns whenever he got involved in a discussion that bogged down.

A few days later he could not seem to make his assistant, Don, understand how he wanted a project to be handled. He realized that he was worried about Don's commitment to the assignment. When he told Don the truth about what he was thinking, the conversation turned into a discussion about how the work needed to be prioritized. Barry noticed that this time telling his own truth seemed to make it easier for Don to speak about his own concerns. Barry continued to experiment, and gradually he learned to be alert for his own concerns and to bring them up early in meetings, especially when discussions started to lag.

What We Don't Discuss Can Hurt Us

Harvard Business School and education professor Chris Argyris observes that unproductive meetings during which people gloss over important information are almost routine in most organizations. He believes that they are the unintentional result of lifelong learning about how to avoid potential threat or embarrassment. We have learned to value control, winning, rationality, and suppressing negative feeling and "to avoid vulnerability, risk, embarrassment, and the appearance of incompetence" (Argyris 1994).

Argyris describes how during many meetings, important topics become undiscussable and what emerge instead are mixed messages that are designed to maintain power and avoid potential threats to certain individuals. To compound the confusion, we are encouraged not to discuss the mixed messages. It is no wonder that many meetings are messy and that telling the truth takes great courage. Yet when people work on discussing the undiscussable, they are better able to share the important information organizations need in order to respond to rapidly changing conditions.

If you think these confusing meetings are the norm, then you are not alone. Most people at meetings react by complying with what they believe to be the expected behavior. We sit in meetings, trying to look interested and thinking of ways we can contribute. Instead we tend to lose interest, feel bored and angry, or develop stress-related symptoms. We develop headaches, upset stomachs, tense muscles, and then we try to relieve the stress by smoking, eating, drinking coffee and alcohol, and paradoxically working harder to try to at least feel productive. We use these and other methods to divert our attention from the important information that we believe is too dangerous to notice or discuss.

Actually it is far more dangerous to your well-being to ignore such information. Research has shown that immune system functioning improves when people routinely use awareness of emotions and sensations to help them determine appropriate actions (Dreber 1996). This awareness is also the first component of emotional intelligence, which psychologist and author Daniel Goleman (1995) claims may be a more important component in your success than your IQ.

Paying Attention to Internal Signals

Waking up is the first step. Becoming aware of how you feel when you are in a confusing situation is critical. Your physical sensations and your emotions provide important information about what is healthy or toxic in your environment. Ignoring these signals is like ignoring the signal lights on the dashboard of your car. Just as your car engine may burn up if you neglect the reminder that it needs oil, you may burn out if you ignore signals of your own discomfort. You cannot do anything useful to manage toxicity if you are unaware of it. Barry's first step in changing his situation was recognizing his own anger.

Once you learn to interpret emotional signals, you can decide what you need to do to take care of yourself. Most of the emotions we experience can be classified as variations on joy, anger, sadness, fear, and shame.

Joy signals that something is going well for you. You do not need to do anything about feeling happy, although some people start to worry (fear) about how they can make the feeling last longer each time they experience it. Others worry that something bad is about to happen, as if there is a magical principle that bad events will inevitably follow good ones. Joy, and every other feeling, will eventually change in response to changing circumstances.

Anger is a natural signal that you are not getting something you want or need. Use this feeling to remind yourself to think about what you want and need in a given situation, and once you have identified what that is, then redirect the angry energy into solving the problem.

Sadness is a natural response to loss. If you know what you have lost, then letting yourself experience the feeling of sadness will eventually help you recover naturally from the loss.

Persistent sadness may actually be a symptom of depression, a condition that often arises when other feelings are ignored or suppressed. If you think you are depressed, consult a mental health professional to determine whether treatment is necessary.

Fear signals real or imagined danger. When you feel afraid, evaluate your situation. If there is real danger, take the steps necessary to protect yourself. If you think you are only imagining danger, you probably need more information about the situation and about yourself. Unrealistic fears often disappear when you examine them or discuss them with others. If you risk telling the truth about your fears, you may find that others share the same fears.

Shame is a feeling that signals a belief that there is something basically wrong with you. This extremely distressing feeling can cause you to react defensively almost instantly. Learning to wait for the feeling to pass and then thinking about what to do next is a useful strategy for managing shame. Sometimes just focusing on breathing slowly and deeply will help this feeling pass more quickly.

Noticing External Signals of Undiscussable Topics

Your internal clues may alert you that a confusing or potentially dangerous problem exists outside yourself. Now the challenge is to spot the tip of the iceberg, so that you can then look for the larger submerged issues. If you notice simple recurring patterns, this should alert you to the presence of organizational defensive routines that are usually used to shield undiscussable information from people's awareness (Argyris 1994).

Signals that defensive routines are being used include repetition, nonresponsiveness, redefinitions, and rapid changing of the subject. These are clues that an issue is not being addressed. They are also subtle signals that are supposed to alter your awareness so you do not notice what has just happened. You usually don't notice these signals, but if you do notice the signals, it would be considered impolite to say anything about them.

Even those who are employing these tactics are usually doing so automatically and outside their conscious awareness. You are supposed to accept the cultural trance of unawareness and maintain the status quo. When you do develop awareness of these patterns *and* skill in disclosing them you risk becoming an empowered leader.

Repetition is perhaps the simplest signal that something is wrong. When someone keeps repeating the same point in a conversation, it often means that the person speaking does not believe that he or she has been heard. It may mean that he or she is searching for some particular response—sometimes your agreement, sometimes your approval. The undiscussable issue may be the speaker's personal desire for contact or acknowledgment.

When a group like Barry's gets stuck in a repetitious argument, it can also mean that there is some other important issue that is not being discussed. Sometimes the relationships and relative power positions among the group members are the hidden issues. At other times, group members are avoiding some obvious topic that they are afraid to address. This kind of avoidance or denial can be likened to no one being willing to talk about the elephant in the living room. Everyone can see it and must take actions to accommodate it, but discussing the elephant is taboo.

Nonresponse is another sign that there is a communication problem. When one person makes a comment and others act as if nothing has happened, then a climate of disrespect is created. When this type of interaction is not discussed, fear of similar disrespect will keep others from voicing their comments, and the hidden issue is kept locked away. The person who risked commenting may feel hurt or angry and respond by withdrawing or by later interfering with the work of the group.

Redefinition is harder for most people to identify. It involves someone responding to a minor detail in a communication but steering away from the more important main point. If you have ever had someone who wanted to discredit you challenge a small detail in a statement you made, while he or she fails to address the more important issue raised by your statement, you know how easy it is to fall into this trap. When Mary asked her manager, Lois, to approve a requisition for more personnel, Lois requested additional information. Weeks went by as Lois demanded more and more details about one aspect of the request, and Mary tried to accommodate her. Meanwhile, the urgent need for more personnel was not approved or even addressed, and Lois's hidden agenda was never disclosed.

Rapid subject changes can also be used to create great confusion and obscure an important, but potentially embarrassing topic. When you are in a conversation and suddenly wonder how on earth you wound up discussing some unrelated topic, suspect this problem. It usually starts with one person describing a complex situation. Another person chooses a detail and starts a conversation about the detail. At this point person three or perhaps person one starts another new conversation based on a detail of person two's narrative. Rarely does the conversation return to any of the earlier subjects. A conversation that spirals out of control sometimes becomes an argument that is hard to resolve, because accusations and counteraccusations come thick and fast, and no one can keep up with them.

Effective Responses to Defensive Routines

1. When you become aware of your own emotional response, tell someone about it. Choose your words carefully and *never* accuse someone else of causing your emotion. You might say, "I notice that I'm feeling increasingly frustrated because..." Be careful to use "I messages" such as "because I thought I would be back at my desk an hour ago."

2. When you realize that you are concerned about something that is being left out of a discussion, voice your concern the way

Barry did: "I've been thinking a lot about . . . , and I'm wondering if anyone else is concerned about this, too." Leave your statement open-ended, rather than putting someone on the spot by asking a direct question. Watch for nonverbal responses such as nods or attempts to hide, and treat them as if they were verbal replies. "Bob, I'm glad to know I'm not alone."

3. When you recognize repetition, call attention to it by acting as if you were responsible for not giving the expected or needed reply. Repeat the point yourself so it will be clear to everyone that you do understand it. "Anne, I think you have said that you are opposed to the plan because . . . Is there something I am missing, or is there something you want me to say about it that I have not said?"

4. When a group gets stuck and repeats the same statements over and over again, say something about being stuck. "We are repeating ourselves. I wonder why we seem to be so stuck." Then either ask for a break or go on with an invitation for everyone present to make a very brief statement about what they are trying to accomplish in the conversation. "I am trying to make sure that we protect the consumer from . . ." or "I am trying to finish this so we can discuss . . ."

5. When a statement you make is ignored, repeat it with the same inflection you used the first time you made it. If your second statement is ignored, say "Excuse me, I just said . . . , and I wonder why nobody responded to me."

6. When a statement someone else makes is ignored, say that you are interested in what the person said. You can either repeat the person's statement or ask him or her to say it again. You can also create space for someone else to speak by saying, "I think that Jack wants to say something."

7. When someone responds to a small detail of what is being presented instead of to the main thrust of your argument, keep track of the central theme, and when the conversation about the detail is complete, bring the conversation back to the main theme. You can say, "Now, can we go back to the discussion of . . ."

8.   When you find yourself lost in a rapidly shifting conversation, acknowledge that you are lost. You can be sure that others are as lost as you are, that they also are wondering what is going on. They will be grateful to you for stopping the action. Do not waste time trying to sort out what happened. Restart the conversation by going back to the original topic, if anyone remembers it. If not, invite each participant to state briefly what he or she would like to have happen in the conversation.

9.   Remember that defensive routines are a common device used to protect everyone from potential embarrassment or discomfort. They are usually not a sinister attempt to cause damage, although they may indeed have a damaging effect. It is important to address difficult topics and bring up important information so that nothing vital will be omitted from the process of making decisions, since flawed decision making can cause major problems for everyone concerned.

References

Argyris, C. "Good Communication That Blocks Learning." *Harvard Business Review* (July–August 1994).

Dreber, H. "Immune Power Personality." *Noetic Sciences Review* 39, (Fall 1996).

CHAPTER

22

Using Agreements to Create Dialogue Instead of Conflict

It is important for any truth teller to realize that your truth is not THE TRUTH, and neither is anyone else's. Exploring different perspectives on the truth instead of arguing about which is correct can best be accomplished in a safe environment. A variety of organizations use an ever-evolving set of agreements to create and maintain a context in which truth-telling can occur.

It is easier to create an argument than it is to create a dialogue. When we have different opinions about the way to solve a problem, we often discuss the alternatives, acting as if there is one correct answer, and our task is to find it. As long as we believe that a single correct course of action exists, we debate the issue. We try to convince each other that a particular position is correct. Someone wins and someone loses. Even when we believe that this is an outmoded way to solve problems, we continue to use it, because it is comfortable and familiar.

A dialogue, by contrast, is an open and frank exchange of ideas for the purpose of seeking mutual understanding. In the original Greek, this term referred to "the free flowing of meaning through a group allowing the group to discover insights not attainable individually" (Senge 1990). Although the dialogue process has been preserved by Native Americans and certain religious groups, for the most part it has fallen into disuse in our competitive culture. The late physicist and philosopher David Bohm explored this idea, and his work led to attempts to reintroduce this process into the world of work.

Practicing the Dialogue Process (Bohm 1990) describes a technology for creating understanding in groups, provides a different way to address diverse perspectives and differences of opinion. According to this definition, dialogue is inclusive instead of exclusive. Dialogue is based on the premise that there are many ways of approaching any issue, and that no single one is correct. The aim of the dialogue process is to create a forum in which ideas can be explored, expanded, deepened, and illuminated until new meaning and understanding emerge. Instead of trying to create support for their own positions, people engaged in dialogue listen to and question each other, attempting to deepen their understanding of all the information being presented.

The principles may be simple, but they are not easy to put into practice. The challenge is to listen with care to each statement or question that is offered, and to respond in a way that deepens the investigation of the topic that is being explored. You may offer a statement of your own understanding or ask a question to focus the exploration in a new area.

Being clear is more important than being right in this mode of discussion. Instead of trying to prove that your idea or position is correct, your task is to explain your beliefs carefully, so that others can understand them. As others come to understand your position, they may ask questions to clarify their understanding or offer observations of their own that will allow you to better understand other aspects of your original ideas. Eventually a shared understanding is developed based on many contributions, and the idea comes to belong to the entire group instead of to any single member of the group.

If it is necessary to make a decision about the issue being addressed, the decision is made after the exploration is completed. Since a common understanding has already been reached, such decisions emerge quickly and easily, without any need to debate different positions. Everyone present has had the opportunity to be heard and acknowledged and has made a contribution to the outcome. Commitment to such decisions tends to be high.

Exploring different perspectives on the truth instead of arguing about which is correct can best be accomplished in a protected environment. Creating such an environment is a process. It takes time to develop the skills of listening deeply and asking questions instead of advocating for your favorite positions. Setting aside uninterrupted time to explore issues without expecting to achieve any particular result and agreeing to simple rules—such as allowing each speaker to complete a statement without interruption— are basic conditions necessary to begin the process. Learning to say, "I wonder what would happen if . . ." instead of "I think we should . . ." is an important part of establishing an environment that promotes dialogue.

An expanded discussion of dialogue can be found in the "Team Learning" section of Peter Senge's groundbreaking book *The Fifth Discipline: The Art and Practice of the Learning Organization* (1990). The Center for Dialogic Communication (see Appendix 1) offers suggestions and training materials for people who wish to explore this process in more depth.

While formally learning and practicing dialogue is an interesting and valuable process, it is time-consuming and requires a great deal of focused attention. Various groups searching for ways to work together harmoniously have evolved practical sets of agreements that can help create an atmosphere where informal dialogue can occur spontaneously.

"Network marketing is a relationship business. The principles in these agreements are so important to us that we won't work with people who won't agree to use them. I use them to provide a foundation for each of my new working relationships," reports Marian Head. She and her partner, Gail Hoag, owners of Changing

Pathways, are independent associates in a network marketing business. In only fifteen months their synergetic teamwork placed them in the top 1 percent of earnings among a group of 160,000 other associates.

Gail and Marian belong to a loosely knit co-creative community, centered in Colorado, that has been developing and living by a set of agreements for over ten years. Members of the community own several successful businesses that are models that others emulate. These agreements, subscribed to freely by each person who joins the business or community activities, create a foundation of trust and safety that supports innovation, creativity, joy, and financial success.

These agreements constitute a living code that helps the community stay focused on creating truthful and caring relationships as the basis for everything they do. Marian reports, "We read our mission statements, objectives, and agreements aloud at meetings at least once a week. It [living by the agreements] is so important to me that I think it [respectful communication] just happens."

History of the Agreements

Sometime in the early 1980s someone in a loose network of friends found a set of agreements on the wall of the Kilgore Trout restaurant in Evergreen, Colorado. The owners of the restaurant had adopted the agreements from an article in *New Realities Magazine* (Brown 1977) about the enormously successful Hawthorne/Stone Real Estate company of San Francisco. Coincidentally, some other members of the group had attended a business workshop that also used the Hawthorne/Stone agreements.

The Hawthorne/Stone agreements are reputed to have been created as "rules of the game" in a business that was introducing the radical (in the mid 1970s) concept of using principles of the heart in a business environment. The agreements were said to be ideas that were tested by the working group to see what impact they would have on the productivity and personal growth of the people involved. Those principles that had a positive effect were retained; the others were discarded.

Glenn Head and several friends decided they needed each other's support to practice using principles of the heart in their businesses. They started meeting regularly to help each other maintain and apply that belief system, and the group evolved into the Geneva Group support community. The members developed a mission statement and used the existing Hawthorne/Stone rules as the basis for developing their own agreements about how to be with each other. The list that follows is an adaptation of the "Geneva Group Agreements," as they existed in Boulder, Colorado, in 1985. Marian Head self-published this list as *rEvolutionary Agreements* in 1991, with the proviso *"Please copy freely and share widely."* This list includes a stated mission; most other variations of these agreements simply state "I agree to the mission of the [blank] group." If you choose to adopt these living and growing agreements, use your own name and mission statement to personalize them.

The Agreements
1.   Commit to the Mission

Our mission is to liberate ourselves and all humanity to realize our full potential. I agree to use this mission as a guide to my actions.

The commitment to a stated mission clarifies the reason any group of people are doing something together. This clarity provides a guideline for the actions of the group. A mission statement must be known and understood for it to be used as a guide for action. There are many guides to creating mission statements that are meaningful. In *The Soul of a Business: Managing for Profit and the Common Good*, Tom Chappell (1993) describes how the mission of Tom's of Maine was created. In the appendix of *First Things First*, Steven Covey (1994) offers a mission statement workshop. Ken Blanchard (1993) also provides useful guidelines for creating meaningful mission statements in *Personal Excellence*.

Once a mission statement is created, it becomes the guiding force for the group. The remaining agreements state the guidelines for how the members of the group will behave with each other while working toward achieving the mission.

2.   Communicate with Integrity

I agree to tell my truth with compassion for myself and others.

My truth, not *the* truth! My truth is a statement of what I believe to be true at the moment. It may be a statement about a passing emotional response, such as "I feel angry when..." Even the act of speaking your truth may change it. Bernie Leibman, psychologist and student of the *Tao Te Ching*, once told me, "People always speak the truth, but sometimes by the time they finish saying it, it is no longer the truth." An agreement to speak your truth gives you and others the opportunity to examine it and explore its meaning.

An exercise from *The Fifth Discipline Fieldbook: Strategies and Tools for Building a Learning Organization*, (Senge et al. 1994) suggests a method of learning to recognize our own unspoken and often hidden truths (p. 246). In the left-hand column exercise, you are asked to reconstruct a troubling conversation and write out the dialogue on the right side of a sheet of paper. Then in the left-hand column you are invited to "write what you were thinking and feeling but not saying." Examining your left-hand column will provide insight about yourself, others, and the choices you make in difficult situations.

Speaking "with compassion for myself" is a stretch for many people. If you tend to tell yourself judgmental things in private that you would never say to another person, because it would be hurtful or demeaning, this is an invitation to change your private conversation. It is an *agreement* not to belittle yourself when you tell your truth to others.

Speaking with compassion for others implies adopting the belief that people are valuable, although their behavior may be unskilled and unpleasant for you. In order to speak with compassion, you must learn to separate the action from the actor, and affirm the actor even if you disagree with the action.

3.   Listen with Your Heart

I agree to listen respectfully to the communication of others and to receive their deepest meaning.

Listening with the intent to learn is a difficult challenge for many people. If you are like most people, you automatically focus on what you plan to say to defend yourself or your beliefs when you feel challenged. When you are thinking about how to respond or defend yourself, you are no longer listening. If you want to develop the discipline of listening until the speaker is finished, try listening carefully so that you can restate what you have heard in your own words. If you restate what you have heard and ask the speaker if you are correct, the speaker will probably experience your respect.

Listening for the truth behind the words that are being spoken takes even more skill and patience. It is hard to avoid thinking judgmental thoughts, and these thoughts block deep understanding. A respected public speaker once said, "I make a daily commitment to not judge others, and occasionally I manage to keep my commitment until noon." The "Mental Models" section of *The Fifth Discipline Fieldbook* (Senge et al. 1994) provides suggestions for developing this skill.

Learning to listen deeply is a challenging task and discipline. As in any discipline, the goal is to practice as diligently as possible, without expectation of becoming 100 percent proficient.

4.   Honor One Another

I agree to acknowledge that everyone, including myself, is making the best possible choice or decision we are capable of at that moment of choice or decision.

Each time you make a choice, many past experiences influence you. They even influence the information you select from the vast pool of external and internal information that is available to you. Your nervous system must screen out far more information than it lets in to keep you from being overwhelmed. Many "logical" decisions are colored by the emotional need to seek pleasure or avoid pain, and what is considered pleasant or painful to you depends on your own personal life experiences. There is no escaping from our humanity, so why not accept it?

5.   Appreciate Your Contributions

I agree to take responsibility for acknowledging myself and receiving acknowledgment from others.

This agreement means noticing your own achievements and inviting others to notice them, too. This is a completely natural procedure we all followed when we were children, by doing things like showing off our artwork and demanding that it be displayed. However, Marian reports that this is one of the most difficult agreements for people to make. The "virtue" of humility is hammered into us when we are children. We are told to wait for others to praise us and to not get a "swelled head." This practice encourages dependency instead of autonomy. Isn't it ironic that the very trait we were taught to suppress as children is one that is valued here?

Acknowledgment from others is a fundamental human need (Berne 1964). Children demand this acknowledgment. Adults may feel guilty or inadequate for even wanting recognition from others, but this does not stop us from needing it. We frequently transfer the responsibility for meeting this need to others, by feeling hurt or angry because they do not acknowledge us. We try to resolve the conflict of needing something we think we should not need by assuming others should automatically know what we need and give it to us.

This agreement legitimizes your need for acknowledgment. It encourages you to reclaim your autonomy and treat yourself the way you want others to treat you.

6.   Express Appreciation for Others' Contributions

I agree to acknowledge others.

This reverses the common practice of ignoring someone while he or she is doing a good job, and then paying attention to the person when he or she makes a mistake. Since all of us thrive on acknowledgment, the old procedure encourages mistakes in order to get recognition. If you express appreciation for something that someone is doing well, he or she will tend to do it more often. (Conversely, if you consistently notice mistakes, the mistakes will also occur more frequently.) If you care about someone, and let the person know, he or she will probably appreciate it. Withholding acknowledgment serves only to reinforce the doubts and negative beliefs people have about themselves. Acknowledgment contributes to trust and growth.

7.   Honor Our Differences

I agree to come from a sense of cooperation and caring in my interactions with others, understanding that our goals are often the same even though our methods of achieving them may differ.

This is another way of looking for the positive intention that lies behind even the most unskilled behavior. In their popular book on negotiation, *Getting to Yes,* Fisher and Ury (1981) use this principle. They teach us that the way to resolve conflict is to start by discovering the individual needs and goals of everyone concerned. Once that is done, a mutually satisfactory way of achieving those goals often quickly emerges.

8. Use Grievances as Opportunities for Growth

I agree to look for unresolved issues within me that may lead me to experience disproportionate reactions to others' behavior.

This agreement covers the times when you respond with rage to an action that others see as mildly annoying, or with tears to a remark that appropriately points out a friend's discomfort with your actions. It is an agreement to search for your own hidden truths and let yourself know what they are, instead of blaming others for your own discomfort.

Your unresolved personal issues are linked to times in the past when you had an intense emotional reaction to something. That something might be a terrifying event like an accident or an assault, or it might be something that others would barely notice, like being laughed at for making a mistake when you were a child. It does not matter whether or not the event was particularly important or even if you remember it. What does matter is that your brain recorded it as so significant that when you encounter a situation that is in any way similar to the earlier event, you automatically react to it.

Your reaction has the emotional intensity of your reaction to the original event. The intensity of your reaction may have little to do with the current event that "caused" it, because your reaction was really caused by the similarity of the current event to the past distressing event, which you may have even forgotten. Your physiology is responsible for your discomfort, not the person who just said something to you!

The methods for decoding this tangle are the same as those described in Chapter 18, "All I Did Was . . . Why Did She React That Way?"

9. Maintain Harmony

I agree to take the time to establish rapport and then to reconnect with anyone with whom I feel out of harmony as soon as it's appropriate.

Harmony is valuable, but not at the expense of being truthful. Grievances and disagreements happen. Nobody is expected to be perfect, and boundaries need to be respected. Honoring this agreement means not holding on to anger at someone who might have acted in a way that caused you difficulty. Instead agree to work out problems and differences in a respectful way.

10. Resolve Problems Constructively

I agree to offer at least one solution anytime I present a problem. I agree to take problems, complaints, and upsets to the person(s) with whom I can resolve them, at the earliest opportunity. I agree not to criticize or complain to someone who cannot do something about my complaint, and I will redirect others to do the same.

When this agreement is put into practice, gossiping and whining are eliminated; so are the common practices of saying negative things to one person about another person and expecting someone else to solve your problems for you. The common games people play are eliminated because everyone agrees to neither support nor rescue victims. If you feel like a victim, you agree to act responsibly anyway.

In practice, if you have a problem with me, you are expected to come to me, tell me about the problem, and suggest at least one solution that would resolve the problem for you. I am expected to honor other agreements by listening to you respectfully and acting to restore harmony.

If, instead of coming to me, you choose to tell someone else about the problem, the other person will remind you that it is your responsibility to take the problem to me. If you do not want to approach me alone, you could ask someone else to help you by either being present at the meeting or by helping you think through various ways of resolving the problem. Then you come to me and discuss the problem with me.

Loren Laureti, an owner of I.T.S., Inc., reports that using this agreement has made a major difference in her telephone equipment installation company. The thirteen-year-old company clarified a new vision and introduced the agreements eighteen months ago. "We have gone from major fault finding about problems to looking within ourselves and talking only with the person who can do something about the problem. Employees used to come to the owners (my ex-husband and myself) and expect us to fix everything. Now if they do that, we redirect them back to the person with whom they are experiencing conflict. Nine out of ten times they can take care of it themselves. Our employees now offer their own solutions to problems and commit to do what they agree to do."

11. Go for Excellence!

I agree to support others and to be supported in participating at the highest levels of excellence.

This means that I will offer and accept challenges to find new and better ways to approach anything. It means that I commit to continue my own personal growth and encourage others to do the same.

12. Learn from Experience

I agree to look for opportunities to learn from my experiences, to continue doing what works and discontinue doing what does not work.

This is an agreement to continuously evaluate the results you achieve through your activities. It is a commitment to acknowledge when a particular behavior is ineffective, and change it. This type of truth-telling requires that you examine familiar and cherished activities and be willing to do something differently, instead of doing what you have always done, simply because that is the way you have always done it.

13. Be a rEvolutionary Leader

I agree to foster an environment of genuine collaboration, in which all people, including myself, feel empowered to express our individual and collective potential.

All of the agreements lead to creating an empowering environment. Focusing on collaboration instead of competition means adopting a belief that there are sufficient resources for you and others to get what you need. Often operating as if this is true helps it become true. When resources are shared instead of hoarded, there is usually more available for everyone.

Another important aspect of a collaborative environment is that appropriate boundaries are created and respected. One way to do this is to make only agreements that you are willing and intend to keep. This means thinking through the implications of an invitation to do something before deciding whether or not to do it. You must feel free to refuse invitations that you feel are inappropriate for you.

Of course, sometimes it is necessary to change an existing agreement. If you know that you cannot keep an agreement in a collaborative environment, it is appropriate to renegotiate it at the earliest possible opportunity. Some groups consider this procedure so important that they include it as a separate agreement in the list.

14.   Reevaluate Your Commitment

I agree to choose and re-choose to participate in this rEvolution. It is my choice.

Substitute the name of your own group or project for rEvolution. Participation in many games or activities means agreeing to operate by the rules that govern those activities. If we choose to play basketball or bridge or even to drive an automobile, we agree to follow certain rules. Participation in a group that uses these agreements as guidelines is also a choice. If we choose to participate, we are choosing to play by these rules. The rules that govern any game can be amended under certain conditions, as can these agreements. They are always subject to revision and evolve by mutual agreement.

15.   Lighten Up!

I agree to create joy in my relationships, my work, and my life.

You can choose to create joy by paying more attention to the positive and entertaining things that happen around you than to the inevitable negative ones. The benefits to you and others abound. Besides reducing stress, strengthening your immune system, and becoming more creative, you become someone that others will enjoy being around. Joy is contagious; spreading it to others makes the world better for everyone.

Loren Laureti thinks that this agreement has been very important for I.T.S. as well. "We used to be very serious around here," she said. "If you slipped up, off with your head! Now we often tell jokes, and we have even bought some Groucho Marx glasses with moustaches. People who are having a difficult day and need to lighten up take them out and wear them."

Resources for Operating by Agreement

These agreements are only a sample of the many different types of agreements groups choose to enter into in order to create a safe environment where truth-telling can occur. The Public Conversations Project of the Family Institute of Cambridge (Massachusetts) also uses a set of ground rules or agreements in its work (Roth 1995). The goal of the group's work "is to transform the quality of conversation among people who have polarized views on issues of public significance." These agreements are listed in Appendix 2.

Organizational trainers and consultants can also help groups to create guidelines that foster truth-telling and clear communication. In *Truth Zone*, consultant Ward Flynn (1996) shares a list of agreements designed to build working relationships. The "Tobacco Agreements" are named to honor the attitudes assumed by the Lakota Sioux Indians during their sacred ceremonial sharing of tobacco. These agreements appear in Appendix 2.

The guiding principles developed by a work team during a training program at the Chicago office of CNA, Inc. are brief and direct.

We will live by the following:

Open, honest communication

Trust, integrity, professional ethics

Respect/courtesy

Accountability

Mutual understanding

Encouragement/positive and constructive feedback

Humor, fun

Tolerance

Forgiveness

Lists of more complex guiding principles that have been used in other organizations appear in Peter Block's *The Empowered Manager: Positive Political Skills at Work* (1987). His information about "putting into words a future we wish to create" is designed to help you build your own "vision of greatness."

It is important to remember that agreements are useful as long as they are actively honored and adhered to. Just writing them and posting them on the wall is not sufficient. In order for your group to create and maintain a safe place where respectful truth-telling can occur, the agreements must serve as active guidelines for your behavior.

Introducing Operating Agreements Invites Changes

Starting to live by these agreements sometimes causes discomfort, when you learn things about yourself or your group that you would rather not know. Loren Laureti reports that I.T.S. lost a number of people who did not want to be part of the team agreements. Although it was painful at the time, she says, "We actually got rid of the deadwood. Those who were not committed to our goals realized that they could not get away with substandard behavior and left."

It has taken time to hire and train new people, but Loren is pleased that the teamwork in the sales department is now beginning to show, and profits are increasing. She has noticed another pleasant and unexpected change: "I used to waste money when people would say they would attend trainings, parties, and special events and then cancel at the last minute. Now people commit to these events and *show up* when they say they will!"

Creating Your Own Operating Agreements

1. Know your mission so that you have a clear understanding of what you are committing to accomplish. If you do not have a mission statement, take the time to create one.

2. Agree to experiment with operating by a number of different agreements.

3. Choose one or two agreements from the lists here or create your own. (One group agreed to stop using profanity.)

4. Decide how long you will practice using these agreements before you evaluate their effectiveness for achieving your purpose.

5. Experiment for the allotted time and then evaluate your results.

6. Decide whether or not to make certain agreements a permanent part of your operating procedure.

7. Choose another agreement or two and repeat the process.

8. Consider making any appropriate agreement with yourself, and using it to guide you in making changes in your personal behavior.

9. Experience the changes that occur and continuously evaluate them.

References

Berne, E. *Games People Play*. New York: Grove Press, 1964.

Blanchard, K. *Personal Excellence*. New York: Simon & Schuster, 1993.

Block, P. *The Empowered Manager: Positive Political Skills at Work*. San Francisco: Jossey-Bass, 1987.

Bohm, D. *On Dialogue*. Ojai, Calif.: David Bohm Seminars, 1990.

Brown, D. "Consciousness in Business." *New Realities Magazine*, 1(3), 1977.

Covey, S., A. R. Merrill, and R. R. Merrill. *First Things First*. New York: Simon & Schuster, 1994.

Chappell, T. *The Soul of a Business: Managing for Profit and the Common Good*. New York: Bantam Books, 1993.

Fisher, R., and W. Ury. *Getting to Yes: Negotiating Agreement without Giving In*. Boston: Houghton Mifflin, 1981.

Flynn, W. *Truth Zone: Building the Truthful Organization from the Bottom Up!* Denver: Matrix Publishing, 1996.

Head, M. *rEvolutionary Agreements.* Boulder Colo.: self-published, 1991.

Roth, S. "From Stuck Debate to New Conversation on Controversial Issues: A Report from the Public Conversations Project." In *Cultural Resistance: Challenging Beliefs about Men, Women, and Therapy,* edited by K. Weingarten. New York: Haworth Press, 1995.

Senge, P. *The Fifth Discipline: The Art and Practice of the Learning Organization.* New York: Doubleday Currency, 1990.

——et al. *The Fifth Discipline Fieldbook: Strategies and Tools for Building a Learning Organization.* Currency, N.Y.: Doubleday, 1994.

23

A Success Story

When Sue found herself in the role of president of the company she and her late husband had started five years earlier, she was overwhelmed. She felt at odds with the whirlwind-paced, crisis-oriented management style her husband had believed was necessary to keep the chaotic business expanding and profitable, but she did not know what else to do. Creating harmony seemed like an impossible dream.

Sue remembered, "When my husband died, the business had been growing fast. There were about fifty employees, things were constantly in chaos, and all I could do was attempt to put out fires. There was little clarity, and people were moving in different directions. Departments made isolated decisions. People blamed each other, guarded their own territories, and often feared retribution if they took the wrong action. I did not know what to do to change the way things were done, and I could not let go. I just wanted to enjoy life and create harmony."

Four years later Sue Wale, president of Malcombs Fresh Re-Pack, enjoys going to work. Her produce repackaging firm, which supplies restaurants, grocery stores, and institutions with prepared produce, now has a synergistic management team and employs a hundred people. "It's like the difference between night and day," Sue reports. "I have learned how to allow the business to grow. We have integrated chaos and harmony. I have become the vision holder, and I allow people who love change and chaos to make it happen. I focus on empowering myself and others, and things become fun and effortless. We support one another, and it is amazing what we can accomplish."

A major step in the transformation occurred several months after her husband's death. Sue was intrigued when consultant Gail Hoag suggested that it was possible to create the harmonious environment that Sue longed for. Gail and her associate, Glenn Head, helped Sue and her vice president identify their own personal visions and a vision for the company.

Sue said, "I had to start being truthful with myself for any real change to happen. The hardest truth was admitting that I didn't want the job of president the way things were then. I began the slow process of redefining my leadership role to become more congruent with who I was and who I was becoming. I felt I would lose trust and respect by stepping outside the typical president's role. Instead I received greater respect, and telling my truth gave others permission to tell their truths too."

When the rEvolutionary Agreements were introduced to the five-member executive team of Malcombs Fresh Re-Pack, the group members chose the ones that seemed appropriate for their company and created a list of team agreements. After using the agreements in the management team for several months, they held another meeting and invited all of the office personnel and warehouse supervisors to take part in the process. All fifteen new people created personal vision statements, and then together the entire staff revised the company vision, mission, and the team agreements.

Their agreement was, "Our purpose is to support, succeed, and excel." This mission statement, twenty individual vision statements, and the team agreements were posted in key places to remind everyone of their commitments. Once that happened "it was like letting go of holding one's breath," Sue said. "We committed to taking responsibility for ourselves, to being honest and respectful, and to bringing our whole selves into the workplace."

Change was slow at first. Three members of the executive team were strongly committed to the company's new direction. One of the two produce buyers felt that he could not adapt to the new ways of doing things. When he told the truth and decided to leave, the other produce buyer joined the majority. Two new members were added to the team, and the problem solving, support, and harmony continued to improve. It even spread to people outside the company.

"Produce buyers for our largest customer used to operate by controlling, manipulating, and making demands of others," Sue remembers. "Our produce buyers stopped tolerating that kind of abusive treatment. When our whole executive team supported our buyers in taking a different stance, the customer gradually got the message. They now have a new set of produce buyers."

One of the things Sue enjoys most now is her freedom to be herself in the company. "My husband and I started Malcombs Fresh Re-Pack together because I wanted to be self-employed, and my husband had a successful career background in produce. It was a good combination then. I didn't have produce knowledge or any background in that field. I'm more interested in supporting others to succeed and excel."

Sue was delighted when one of the executives on the team admitted that he had always wanted to run his own business. She believes that he would have left the company if he had not been encouraged to be truthful about his aspirations. Sue said, "He has not had to leave. Now he leads major areas of this company, and we can focus together on empowering others who excel in their own areas to do their best for all of us. Many long-term employees are still with me and have helped the company come through difficult times."

Sue's current challenge is to introduce the team agreements to all of the company employees. She feels challenged because Malcombs Fresh Re-Pack employees speak several different languages. She is certain that she will find a way to make it happen, nonetheless. For now she is pleased that "everything works better when I recognize and acknowledge my own strengths and purpose and support others in doing the same thing. People who tell the truth seem to just be drawn to the right positions at the right time.

I focus on the essence of personal growth and harmony, and the form is left to the individuals who do know what they are doing. They are every bit the decision makers, and it takes all of us to run this company. Things become much more effortless, and we get on with creating our common dreams. We all focus on being truthful to ourselves when we walk through the front door. The core of it all is being honest with myself and being honest with others."

EPILOGUE

Once upon a time, a long time from now, an emperor who loved clothes was approached by two con men who made him an offer he refused. They promised to weave him a special cloth that would be invisible to any who were stupid or unworthy of their positions. The emperor told them that he could think of no reason that such cloth would be of any use to him.

The emperor politely explained that in his empire anyone who did not feel competent to fulfill the requirements of his or her position would say so immediately and either resign or get the help that was needed to fulfill his or her duties. Furthermore, the emperor explained that after eons of research, the sages of the empire had concluded that there were no stupid people. By now, everyone understood that unskilled behavior simply indicated that someone needed additional help, which was readily available and always supplied.

The two con men exchanged puzzled glances and left the empire. Some said they were looking for greener pastures—a place where people were not yet wise and willing to learn.

AFTERWORD

Empowerment Systems, the business that my husband and I share, has provided consultation and cutting-edge tools for individuals and organizations since 1972. Our passion is to coach our clients to develop productive, creative, and synergistic relationships. Truth-telling is integral to this process. My purpose in writing *What Is the Emperor Wearing? Truth-Telling in Business Relationships* is to start a conversation. It's time to talk about creating relationships and organizational systems where the truth can be told.

Please send me (preferably by e-mail) your comments, stories, and questions about truth-telling successes and learning experiences. Interesting selections will be posted to our Empowerment Systems Web site, so the conversation can expand to include others.

I am particularly eager to hear from business owners and executives who are challenging themselves to create truth-telling cultures in their own companies.

Empowerment Systems offers executive coaching and consultation in person and by phone. Seminars, workshops, and talks for groups of any size are also available. Contact our office for details.

Laurie Weiss
Empowerment Systems
506 West Davies Way
Littleton, CO 80120
(303) 794-5379
(800) 484-5846, PIN #2445
Fax: (303) 794-5408
e-mail: weiss@empowermentsystems.com
Web site: http://www.empowermentsystems.com

APPENDIX
1

Information Resources

For publications, computer conferencing, seminars, and study groups:

The Intuition Network
369-B Third Street, #161
San Rafael, CA 92901
Phone: (415) 256-1137
Fax: (415) 456-2532
e-mail: intuition.network@intuition.org

For audiotapes, publications, and seminars about dialogue:

The Center for Dialogic Communication
23010 Lake Forest Drive, #274
Laguna Hills, CA 92653
Phone: (800) 927-2527, ext. 9776

For materials on creating dialogue between people polarized on intense emotional issues:

Sallyann Roth
The Public Conversations Project of the Family Institute of Cambridge
46 Kondazian Street
Watertown, MA 02172
e-mail: sroth@world.std.com or thepcpteam@aol.com

To find an international network of competent and caring professionals who are committed to helping others learn to communicate honestly and skillfully, contact:

International Transactional Analysis Association
450 Pacific Avenue, Suite 250
San Francisco, CA 94133-4640
Phone: (415) 989-5640
Fax: (415) 989-9343
e-mail: itaa@itaa-net.org
http://www.itaa-net.org

APPENDIX

2

Additional Agreements That Facilitate Truth-Telling

The "Tobacco Agreements"[1]

1. *Talk straight.* Establish rapport. Communicate your intention to be in relationship—work together—and be of service.

2. *Take care of old business.* Clear up any old business that may affect the relationship and the ability for either party to fully participate in the task at hand.

3. *Be clear on the details.* Seek a deep and thorough understanding of the details available to the other person. This person is your customer—be proactive in seeking information.

[1] From W. Flynn, *Truth Zone: Building the Truthful Organization from the Bottom Up!* [Denver: Matrix Publishing, 1996]. Matrix Publishing, 10750 Irma Drive, Suite 11, Denver, CO 80233-3630; Fax: (303) 443-8143; e-mail: wflynn@truthzone.com; Web site: http://www.truthzone.com

4. *Accurately reflect back what you understand.* Repeating the details before beginning the task assures both parties that everything that has been communicated was complete and understood.

5. *Establish conditions for your participation.* Before jumping into the task at hand, consider your ability to fulfill the request. Can you do it? Do you have needs? Do you have the authority, information, tools, time, and support necessary to do what is being requested? Make certain your needs are heard and understood.

6. *Communicate the hard truths.* Do you have the right to refuse the task? Can you tell the other person (whether it is your boss or a coworker) how that person's performance affects the project? Likewise, will you get honest ongoing feedback about your own performance?

7. *Do an overview of the agreement and relationship.* Conclude the meeting with a summary. It spells out the details of the agreement for both parties and ends with an acknowledgment of the current state of the relationship.

Proposed Ground Rules for Meetings Between People in Conflict and People Separated by Silence[2]

Dialogue between people in conflict with each other and people separated from each other by silence can be fostered by ground rules that promote a culture of respect and reciprocal interest while discouraging a culture of isolation or divisiveness. The facilitator can propose ground rules or agreements that have proved useful before, while inviting and staying open to modifications and additions from present participants.

Ground rules (agreements) that have been reliably useful include the following:

[2] Adapted from materials of The Public Conversations Project of the Family Institute of Cambridge. Copyright © January, 1996 Sallyann Roth, 46 Kondazian Street, Watertown, MA 02172. Revised June 1996.

1. *Confidentiality.* Can we agree that all that happens or is spoken of in this meeting is confidential; that is, we will not speak about specifics, even in a disguised form, without the express permission of participants. Whatever confidentiality agreement is made will be revisited at the end of the meeting, so that people can tighten, loosen, or otherwise alter parts of the agreement. In any case, the most conservative wish will hold, and no change will occur without the agreement of all people present.

2. *Freedom to pass.* "Pass" if you are unready or unwilling to speak at any time. This means that you may choose not to answer a question or not to follow a suggestion when you are not ready or willing to do so. You need not give any explanation. You can "pass for now" or just pass. A "pass" decision is not only a respectworthy option; it establishes the meeting context as a noncoercive one and is seen as a help.

3. *The right of self-definition.* Can we agree to use respectful language (e.g., to only use descriptors for each other that the others would use about themselves)?

4. *No interrupting.* Can we agree to allow others to finish their thought before responding, that is, to avoid interrupting?

5. *Represent only one's self.* Can we all agree to speak only for ourselves, that is, not to talk about what "we," "you," or "they" think and feel?

6. Genuine inquiry rather than "knowing" (questions of genuine curiosity):

    A. Questions, not attributions

    B. Clarification, not assumptions

    C. Personal speaking and inquiring, not persuasion

Can we agree that when we are tempted to attribute thoughts and feelings to others that those others have not specifically said were their own thoughts and feelings, or when we are tempted to make assumptions about the other, or to persuade the other to a "side," that we will retreat from a "knowing" position by refusing to attribute, assume, or persuade, and instead that we will ask questions of the other to learn how the other would self-describe, to clarify what the other is trying to show or to say, to learn how come the other might think, feel, act, as he or she does?

7. *Focusing.* Can we agree to maintain a central focus at any one time and to avoid side conversations?

8. *Sharing time.* Can we agree to agree to work together to see that we share "air time," or conversational space, fairly?

BIBLIOGRAPHY

Anonymous. *Twelve Steps and Twelve Traditions*. New York: Alcoholics Anonymous World Services, 1953.

Argyris, C. *Strategy, Change, and Defensive Routines*. Boston: Pitman, 1985.

——"Good Communication That Blocks Learning." *Harvard Business Review* (July–August 1994).

Benson, H. *The Relaxation Response*. New York: Morrow, 1975.

Berne, E. *Games People Play*. New York: Grove Press, 1964.

Blanchard, K. *Personal Excellence*. New York: Simon & Schuster, 1993.

Blanchard, K., and S. Johnson. *The One Minute Manager*. New York: Morrow, 1982.

Bohm, D. *On Dialogue*. Ojai, Calif.: David Bohm Seminars, 1990.

Brown, D. "Consciousness in Business." *New Realities Magazine* 1, no. 3 (1977).

Chappell, T. *The Soul of a Business: Managing for Profit and the Common Good*. New York: Bantam Books, 1993.

Covey, S., A. R. Merrill, and R. R. Merrill. *First Things First*. New York: Simon & Schuster, 1994.

Dreber, H. "Immune Power Personality." *Noetic Sciences Review* 1996, no. 39.

Fisher, R., and W. Ury. *Getting to Yes: Negotiating Agreement without Giving In*. Boston: Houghton Mifflin, 1981.

Flynn, W. *Truth Zone: Building the Truthful Organization from the Bottom Up!* Denver: Matrix Publishing, 1996.

Goleman, D. *Emotional Intelligence*. New York: Bantam Books, 1995.

Hayakawa, S. I. *Language in Thought and Action*. San Diego: Harcourt Brace, 1949.

Head, M. *rEvolutionary Agreements*. Boulder Colo.: self-published, 1991.

Janis, I. L. *Victims of Groupthink*. Boston: Houghton Mifflin, 1972.

Kabat-Zinn, J. *Wherever You Go, There You Are*. New York: Hyperion, 1994.

Karpman, S. B. "Script Drama Analysis." *Transactional Analysis Bulletin* 7, no. 26 (1968): 39–43.

Kinsley, J., ed. *The Poems and Songs of Robert Burns*. Oxford: Clarendon, 1968.

Kornfield, J. *Buddha's Little Instruction Book*. New York: Bantam Books, 1994.

LaBorde, G. Z. *Influencing with Integrity: Management Skills for Communication and Negotiation*. Palo Alto, Calif.: Syntony Publishing, 1984.

LeShan, L. L. *How to Meditate; A Guide to Self-Discovery*. Boston: G. K. Hall, 1974.

Luft, J. *Group Process: An Introduction to Group Dynamics*. Palo Alto, Calif.: National Press, 1963.

Maslow, A. H. *Motivation and Personality*. New York: Harper & Row, 1970.

Mitchell, S., trans. *Tao Te Ching: A New English Version*. New York: Harper & Row, 1988.

Peters, T. J. *Thriving on Chaos: Handbook for a Management Revolution*. New York: Knopf, 1987.

——"Tom Peters Live." Audiotape. Boulder, Colo.: Career Track Publications, 1991.

Roth, S. "From Stuck Debate to New Conversation on Controversial Issues: A Report from the Public Conversations Project." In K. Weingarten, ed., *Cultural Resistance: Challenging Beliefs about Men, Women, and Therapy*. New York: Haworth Press, 1995.

Schiff, J., and A. Schiff. "Passivity." *Transactional Analysis Journal* 1, no. 1 (1971): 71–78.

Senge, P. *The Fifth Discipline: The Art and Practice of the Learning Organization*. New York: Doubleday Currency, 1990.

Senge, P., et al. *The Fifth Discipline Fieldbook: Strategies and Tools for Building a Learning Organization*. Currency, New York: Doubleday, 1994.

Sher, B. *Wishcraft*. New York: Viking Press, 1979.

——*I Could Do Anything If I Only Knew What It Was*. New York: Delacorte Press, 1994.

Simon, S. "Forgiveness." Workshop presented at National Conference on Addictions, Colorado Springs, Colo., August 25, 1987.

Sinetar, M. *To Build the Life You Want, Create the Work You Love*. New York: St. Martin's Press, 1995.

VanVogt, A. E. *The World of A*. New York: Simon & Schuster, 1948.

Wagner, A., and D. Wagner. *The Diversity Formula*. London: The Industrial Society of London, 1997.

Weiss, L. *I Don't Need Therapy, But . . . Where Do I Turn for Answers?* Deerfield Beach, Fla.: Health Communications, 1991.

Weiss, L., and J. Weiss. *Recovery from Co-Dependency: It's Never Too Late to Reclaim Your Childhood*. Deerfield Beach, Fla.: Health Communications, 1989.

INDEX

Laurie Weiss discovered that there isn't any TRUTH when she was 15 years old and was first exposed to the insights of General Semantics. Learning that we create our reality, our truth, by the language we use to express our thoughts and experiences transformed her understanding of the world. She was appalled to realize the amount of conflict created by people who believe they have THE TRUTH, and that they should impose it on others. Her lifelong commitment to exploring and sharing the implications of this idea led her to develop an unusual array of professional and personal skills and interests.

She holds a Ph.D. in Health and Human Services from Columbia Pacific University, and is certified as a Teaching and Supervising Transactional Analyst in Clinical, Organizational, and Educational fields. She has served the International Transactional Analysis Association in many capacities, including ten years on the Ethics Committee, educating professionals, and researching and helping resolve ethical issues. Dr. Weiss and her husband/business partner, Jonathan B. Weiss, Ph.D., have worked together since 1972, making many professional presentations throughout the U.S. and eight other countries.

As a non-traditionally trained therapist, coach and consultant, she has specialized in facilitating the development of healthy, synergistic relationships in business, professional, and personal settings. She helps people resolve conflict by leading them to discover their own truths and communicate them respectfully to others.

She is author of *I Don't Need Therapy, But . . . Where Do I Turn for Answers?* and *An Action Plan for Your Inner Child: Parenting Each Other*, and is co-author of *Recovery from Co-Dependency: It's Never Too Late to Reclaim Your Childhood.* Her numerous articles have appeared in publications as diverse as *The Training and Development Journal, Woman's Business Chronicle, Choices Magazine, Transactional Analysis Journal,* and addiction and recovery publications.